Where did we GO WRONG

A Question Concerning Marital Struggles, Conflicts, & Triumphs

I0458232

All inquirers should be addressed to:

Book Savvy International Inc.
PMB 428 1751 Colorado Blvd. Los Angeles, CA 90041

Hotline: (213) 855-4299
https://booksavvyinternationalinc.com/

Ordering Information:
Amount Deals. Special rebates are accessible on the amount bought by corporations, associations, and others. For points of interest, contact the distributor at the address above.

Printed in the United States of America.

ISBN-13   Paperback   979-8-89190-229-9
          eBook   979-8-89190-228-2

Library of Congress Control Number: 2024921592

Where did we
GO WRONG

A Question Concerning Marital
Struggles, Conflicts, & Triumphs

REV. DR. LORENZA JAMES

Book Savvy International Inc.

Preface

Where did we go wrong? Where do we go from here? These challenging questions are often found attached to couples experiencing difficulties in their marriages. Before divorce becomes the final word in their relationships, couples are encouraged to examine their interest, motives, commitment, and personal investment to determine whether their marriages may be restored or maintained. Marriage is a sacred relationship institution. It is ordained by God and intended to be a bonding and binding lifetime connection. Men and women who seek lifetime partners in which to build their lives should know and understand that marriage is not an isolated building process. There are loving and supporting family, friends, and acquaintances who are willing and available to provide support and encourage positive marital development. The strength and weakness as well as the lasting or failure of marriages hinge on these four elements: Communication, Finances, Sex and Intimacy, and Family and Friends. Through each of these categories, couples must assess the proper use of them for their marital success. Where did we go wrong? Is quitting an option? Is staying cowardice? Will divorce provide relief? Or will it bring emptiness and loneliness? Couples must decide whether their relationships and marriages are worth them investing the necessary time and understanding to intimately answer the question, Where Did We Go Wrong?

Acknowledgement

This book is dedicated to married couples everywhere who after facing many opportunities to leave their relationships, instead decided to stay together, mend their brokenness, and with love work through their issues, concerns, and disappointments.

To Mrs. Deborah Harris James, the most beautiful and loving woman I could have chosen to be my wife or God could have given me as a marital partner. Our marriage has carried us through 50 years of love, challenges, and heart-felt commitments. Her encouragement has been my strength and motivation to strive for excellence and reach my desired goals.

During our 50 years of marriage God blessed us with five exceptional children: Lorenza II (Atom who died 12-23-2023), Michael, Rachael, Amy, and Matthew. Eight grandchildren: Lorenza III (Trey), Kieamber, Michael II, Makenna, Alexis, Matthew II (MB), Zoe, and Paxton. One great grandchild, Nairobi (Anna). Son-in-law Jeremiah Brown.

Contents

Introduction

"Marriage or Divorce"

Five years ago, George Wilson married Sandy Smith, the woman he called "love of my life." Their marriage began happily. The joy of their relationship was them spending time together. In five years of marriage, their home, bed, and life were all examples of a couple expressing love for each other. However, after five years of marriage they began drifting apart. Their main interests were no longer in each other. Their focus had turned to doing separate activities with other people. They failed to notice how subtle their lives were moving away from one another. Their movements from each other became disguised as giving room for personal interests. Their relationship became an isolated meeting here, or an unscheduled event there. Because of their supposed evolving schedules, they would leave home early mornings and come back home late nights. It was obvious from their actions that they were heading toward separation. Soon their idle times and times from each other made room for their hearts and minds to wander. Unfortunately, when they became aware of how distant their relationship had become it was too late to restore a marriage spoiled by lost time and unshared love. Because the relationship had reduced itself to constant arguments, name calling, and humiliating discussions, divorce became the end of this once promising loving marital relationship.

This morning was sad for George who found himself waking up alone and lonely. His beloved wife Sandy was gone. Her empty space in the bed made him feel worse. When she decided to leave the marriage, his world was turned upside down. Her leaving him was not an impulsive or last-minute decision. It was not an overnight surprise. George was aware that much of the blame for their marital failures rested on him. It was his actions, attitude, and lack of consideration for Sandy's feelings, opinions, and input into the marriage which caused her to give up on the marriage, pack her bags, and leave their home. Perhaps if he had given her more of his attention or complimented her efforts to make him happy, she may have been willing to stay and work things out. Instead, she was gone. George realized that it was because of his selfishness that Sandy was gone. He had taken both she and their relationship for granted.

Marital troubles which invaded their five-year marriage caused them much consternation as they struggled to keep love and respect in their relationship. Time after time and day after day, as much as they tried to make things work, their efforts only made their lives miserable. Instead of sharing a love which would build happiness and draw them closer together, they could only find fault with each other. This caused their once love-filled marriage to melt down into being nothing more than negative emotions, dissension, bitterness, and lack of trust. The finger-pointing by each of them for the calamity which their marriage had become brought no resolve to the emotional conditions of their home. There was enough blame for each of them to shoulder the breakup. George, being the man of his house, could have taken responsibility for the marriage dissolving to the level and condition in which they agreed to part ways. Instead, he took the spotlight off himself and pointed the finger at his wife. He blamed Sandy for the relationship falling apart so that his negative attitude and disruptive behaviors would not be considered reasons for separation.

The major problem in their marriage was that George lost interest in Sandy. He had come to feel trapped in a marriage he longer wanted. He wanted to end the marriage. Get out of it. Therefore, he started mistreating Sandy in small and insensitive ways to upset her and steer her interest towards some other person. To his surprise his plan worked perhaps better and quicker than he expected. One day when Sandy left her cell phone unattended George explored her text messages to see who she may be communicating with. He found several suspicious and very personal text messages. His warm and affectionate care for Sandy changed when he read the messages from one of her male coworkers. His discovery of Sandy's perceived infidelity made him angry. It also caused him to feel inferior to whoever this person was who had stolen his wife's attention away from him. What was wrong with him? He questioned himself. Did he not meet her satisfaction? His insecurity built up such rage within him that all he wanted to do was to make her hurt as he was feeling hurt. He had forgotten that it was he who started this lost-love process when his interest in Sandy changed and he secretly desired to be rid of her.

The information in her phone shocked him. Instead of talking with Sandy about his suspicions, he began accusing her of cheating on him. Living with him became intolerable for Sandy. George's persistent efforts to prove that Sandy had been cheating wouldn't allow Sandy to give any reasons for the text messages in her phone. He offered no room for understanding this marital violation. No explanation she gave removed his conclusion about her being unfaithful. Therefore, George used his suspicions as reasons to harass Sandy through accusations, surveillances, and made-up stories. These manipulative activities became daily personal attacks on Sandy's character, the woman he promised to love and vowed to support. After a period of enduring insults, humiliations, and accusations, Sandy decided to leave the marriage. She needed peace. She needed to restore her own self-esteem.

Regardless of what explanations Sandy gave to assure George that his accusations were false, he never believed her. His way of thinking was that Sandy being a married woman should not have any kind of intimate relationship, including text messages, with any man other than her husband. George believed that Sandy's referring to her coworker as just a friend was used as cloaking for what they were really doing. He was convinced that being with that other person meant she was cheating. He readily assumed that Sandy was using the same method as he to avoid being caught cheating. His way of covering up his escapades with other women had been to call them his friends. Regardless, George continued to speak and say unkind words to Sandy. He called her all kinds of self-defeating names, including vulgar, profane, and slang street words to break her down. Although Sandy tried to stay at her house because she valued being married, she couldn't. Living under such debasing conditions had damaged her self-esteem. After Sandy had taken as much as she could, she decided to leave George. As she gathered some of her personal items and clothing, George threatened her with the word she thought would never be part of her marital relationship, DIVORCE! He said to her that if she leaves to never again think about coming back to the house or marriage.

Divorce is what this marriage had come to. On this day of absolution George had mixed emotions. Impulsively, he had asked for it. Still, he dreaded that his marriage had come to this decision. The noisy sounds of his alarm clock awakened him to the sadness of this day. In the process of getting dressed, questions clouded his thinking. Was divorce what he really wanted or needed? Did the five years of marriage mean anything? Did he really mean to say those horrible and debasing words he shouted at Sandy? What happened to the beautiful life, home, and promising future their marriage was supposed to become? Questions without answers. Everything had changed. Love had turned into regret, kindness had become bitterness, peace had been replaced by anger, and marriage being a sacred union had become an uncaring relationship. Everything had changed. Five years ago, George and Sandy stood before God at the altar of matrimony. The church filled with many witnesses heard them through endearing tears vow to love each other until death. Well death came to them on this day. Not that either one of them physically died, rather, on this day their relationship ended. Their marriage died. Divorce won this battle leaving them to answer this one question, "Where did we go wrong?"

A QUESTION OF DIVORCE

Where did we go wrong? This question has haunted many couples whose loving marriages turned from positive to negative and ended in divorce. Disappointment became an under-statement for many of these couples whose glamourous images of marriages failed to live up to their expectations. They found themselves participating in divorce procedures. Ironically, many couples who enter this marital engagement have love, joy, peace, and happiness as being their long-term relational expectations. Unfortunately, some couples who dream of long-lasting relationships regretfully have theirs end in divorce. Many reasons contribute to marriages coming to this decision, including unfaithfulness, infidelity, deceits, lies, and betrayals. Such disappointments of these shattered relationships often leave couples wondering why things didn't work out. Why is it that the love they so highly sought and valued evaporated like water from their hearts and blowing away like leaves in the wind? Although some couples, in dissolving relationships, try to stay together or hold on to their marriages for appearance's sake, living with the pains, hurts, and regrets of unreturned love and empty embraces often move relationships to divorce.

Divorce is a halting word filled with negative feelings of bitterness, hatred, resentment, and disappointments. Divorce involves couples coming to fatal decisions which end marriages. It is the final action that troubled marriages reach to end their agreement to remain together. Getting divorced is for some couples a relief, but for others an embarrassment. Marriage for those with regrets recalls their dream which was supposed to be their love story. Instead, it turned out to be for many couples unproductive and regretful relationships. Marriage and divorce! What do these relational entities tell others about relationships? What can be learned by their stories? What relationship dangers can be avoided by their examples? Who is willing to expose their failed marriages to the judgment of others? Who is willing to relive the marital struggles they endured, the agonies, pains, rejections, and sorrows that caused divorce to be the final word? Such a couple named and called into the examination spotlight will be Peter and Gloria.

Peter and Gloria were newlyweds who learned that being married was not always like a bed of roses, or perhaps that's exactly what marriage is. As with the rose being a beautiful portrait of love surrounded by thorns capable of inflicting pain when not properly handled, so are marital relationships. When couples love each other, their embraces become loving portraits of beauty. However, the thorns in these relationships represent marital difficulties and hardships. Peter and Gloria's marriage, like George and Sandy's, struggled for survival. They too faced the marital question, where did we go wrong? However, unlike George and Sandy, they were willing to try and answer the question before reaching the dreadful conclusion of divorce. The lives of many couples portrayed will figurately represent all couples who wrestle with martial issues and for a solution make divorce their consideration. Peter and Gloria began their marriage with much love and adoration for one another. It seemed that nothing would change them or what they shared together. However, as with all marriages, there will be issues, concerns, problems, and even troubles which will test the strength and endurance of such relationships. After a short period of glee, Peter and Gloria experienced sever marital problems. Such events turned their storybook union filled with nice and kind expressions into contentious discussions. These interactions brought on a decline in their relationship and moved them from being loving and caring to being defensive and mean-spirited to one another. Their endearing love and communication had diminished to the point where they were willing to settle for either separation or divorce. Yet, they held out hope for a better outcome.

Realizing that divorce was a final act, Peter and Gloria reasoned within themselves that perhaps that there was something that they could have or should have done to change this finality. Self-examination for them became opportunities to assess the impact their actions had on their marriage. Despite all the negatives that their marriage experienced, they realized that if they pursued hope without being critical or judgmental of each other, their marriage had a chance to work. Their willingness to seek positive results for their marriage encouraged them to honestly ask themselves and each other this vital question, "Where Did We Go Wrong?"

PETER AND GLORIA

Peter and Gloria became husband and wife five years ago. Their wedding ceremony was picturesque. It was truly a gala affair. The environment around their ceremony was filled with joyful expressions. The total atmosphere spoke openly and genuinely of their love. It appeared to everyone at the ceremony that this couple was perfectly made for each other. If paradise, the oasis of perfection, needed a symbol of beauty in love, and a genuine relationship, this couple was the right display. However, their union was not without distinction. It was their need to be loved that drew them together. It was the love that they found in each other that kept them together. From the moments they were drawn together, they loved each other, laughed out loud together, and shared the thrill of being in each other's company. Things were going storybook well for them until one day they began noticing slight disruptions in their shared times together. A few distractions in their focused attention toward each other. Undiscussed changes occurred in their relationship. What was happening with them? What was going on in their love relationship? These questions challenged them to personally investigate the strengths and weaknesses of their marriage. They became aware that the glow, joyful expressions, and happy shared moments which defined their love had been replaced with relational distancing, silence instead of conversations, less outing engagements together, and less romantic times.

Peter and Gloria learned that every married couple goes through some kind of marital gauntlet. They struggle to understand one another, strive to live peacefully together, work hard to keep love in their hearts, and do their best to avoid making divorce the final word spoken. Peter and Gloria love story mimicked the challenges and marital difficulties every married couple wrestle to overcome.

MARRIAGE UNDERSTOOD

Marriage, ordained by God as an institution with the purpose of joining men and women in lifelong relationships. Marital connections are both physical and spiritual. Marriage is not a one-size-fit-all successful engagement. Marriage is a couple directed work in progress. Therefore, every couple seeking this sacred union should be counseled on the impactful meaning of marriage and its requirements. Marital understanding is essential to couples attaining marital harmony. Marriage is a serious engagement and couples in love should trust it for security and not treat it as an experiment. Living together before should not be viewed as an alternative solution. No! This is not the correct understanding of marriage, engagement, or commitment.

Couples during marital counseling should become aware of each one's responsibility in making this life impacting decision. Marital emphasis on required duties, cooperation, and expectations should cause couples to envision them living together beyond the pageantry of their wedding ceremonies. Their focus, interest, and understanding of marital relationships should be about knowing how to build a loving home environment. They should know that marriage is a sacred bond which must be approached or engaged with understanding of what is required of each partner. In this way when marital troubles, problems, or seemingly uncompromising issues become active players in the marriage, couples should not be willing to discard their marriages by making divorce their solution.

Divorce, for some couples, is a hurtful word. It is for some other couples a word of relief. Regardless of which category of marital separation, divorce remains a word signifying incompletion. When divorce comes at the end of troubled marriages, it usually does not end the troubled relationship. What it often does is leave couples with many unresolved issues, needed adjustments, and questions without answers. It also leaves these separated couples with needed spiritual healing and personal restoration. Divorce becomes a constant reminder to couples of their broken promises to love their chosen partners forever. Divorce is not how most couples expect their marriages to end. Yet when relationships reach irreconcilable differences, often divorce is the sad conclusion many couples must accept.

When divorce happens, couples are forced to examine the faults and flaws of their failed relationships. The most common question usually asked of and by couples is 'What happened?' Perhaps the more accurate question that should be addressed after relationships fail is 'Where did we go wrong?" This question becomes essential for couples seeking ways and understanding as to how broken relationships may be restored. On the other side of the coin, couples who have become tired of being married are not interested in maintaining any kind of relationship with that spouse. They care less about evaluating their failed marriages. Many such couples often feel that the sooner the ordeal ends the better. For them, divorce was not only the right decision, but it was also the best decision to make. Deciding to divorce prevents them from pretending to love while living miserably and continuing down this unpleasant marital road. Marriage for them had been nothing less than a journey filled with despair. Let it be noted that all marriages have problems, bumps in the road, drastic, and sometimes even dramatic confrontations. In almost all cases there is an urge by participating couples to give up and quit. However, when couples give themselves time for reflections, they find reasons not to quit. When they consider the wholeness of their marriages, they learn how precious and valuable their relationships can become.

Quitting is a false platform for success. Its quick solutions rarely provide the expected joy, comfort, peace or happiness desired. So, when couples in troubled marriages are counseled to believe that quitting would be better than working through issues, they often end up feeling betrayed by such guidance. For those who followed this wary-minded counseling, they discovered that quitting failed to provide them relief from their marital agonies. It didn't give them the mental freedom needed to move forward with their lives. Quitting as described in poet Edgar Guest's poem, "Don't Quit" offer encouraging words which challenge differences between emotional and practical decision making.

"Don't Quit"

When things go wrong, as they sometimes will,
When the road you're trudging seems all uphill,
When the funds are low and the debts are high,
And you want to smile, but you have to sigh,
When care is pressing you down a bit
Rest if you must, but don't you quit.

Life is queer with its twists and turns,
As everyone of us sometimes learns,
And many a failure turns about,
When they might have won, had they stuck it out.
Don't give up though the pace seems slow,
You may succeed with another blow.

Often the goal is nearer than,
It seems to a faint and faltering man,
Often the struggler has given up,

When he might have captured the victor's cup;
And he learned too late when the night came down,
How close he was to the golden crown.

Success is failure turned inside out,
The silver tint of the clouds of doubt,
And you never can tell how close you are,
It may be near when it seems so far.
So stick to the fight when you're hardest hit,
It's when things seem worst that you must not quit.

Those determined to end marriages considered broken beyond repair are willing to accept divorce as relief. Divorce sometimes provides such couples with the illusion that changing partners will fill their loneliness and emptiness. Often, they soon discover that this deceit was nothing more than wishful thinking. Couples who decide to end their marriages through divorce need recovery time before engaging in new love interests. By nature, human beings need healing time when any parts of the body are broken. Time is required when humans heal from brokenness, including physical, mental, spiritual, and psychological damages. When divorced couples do not give themselves time to heal before starting new relationships, they often take the pains of their past failures with them. That is why hurt people should not be anxious to start new loves without allowing healing and recovery to take place. Otherwise, they will remain victims to their own hurts, disappointments, and bad judgments. When couples out of broken marriages continue to look for true love through the windowpanes of hearts damaged by hurt, pain, poor judgment, or bad decision, they will repeat this vicious circle of doubts and regrets.

Some couples in failed marriages desire to quit the relationships and start over with someone else. However, the dangers of quitting one relationship to begin another often reveal individuals' instability, lack of trust, and belief that marriage is no longer sacred. Therefore, it is important for divorced couples to give themselves time for mental and emotional adjustments to avoid again being in bad marriages. However, before divorce becomes the final act in marriages, couples should be willing to do their best to maintain their homes and lives together. Friends and loved ones' advice and opinions must be cautiously considered. Although these friends and loved ones may genuinely care, they can become short-sighted enablers providing untimely advice or wrong solutions. Such advice is often given by friends and loved ones lacking full knowledge of couples' occurrences in the marriage. Incomplete awareness of marital situations could yield advice centered on feelings without considering numerous mistakes couples make in their marriages.

On the proverbial side of the bed, couples should not be encouraged to remain in unhealthy or unsafe marital confines for the sake of being married. Couples forced or coerced by anyone to remain in marriages for appearances sake usually experience several forms of abuse. Therefore, couples who are ill-fitted together, or biblically stated, "unequally yoked together," must not be forced or encouraged to remain in or endure torturous relationships. In such settings, when couples feel forced to stay together for reasons other than being in love, they will ultimately come to resent one another. Without shared love, couples are ill-equipped to build homes, marriages, or relationships together.

One of the most important marital acts for couples to do is to build each other up and not tear one another down. Marriage is a loving bond of support and encouragement. It is not a relationship filled with ridicule and rejections. The more married couples grow together, the less likely they are to be caught up in romantic rollercoasters or merry-go-rounds circles doing things without purpose or destination. Perhaps the 1972 rhythm and blues song by the Stylistics from Philadelphia, Pennsylvania, 'Break Up to Make Up' best describes such emotionally drained couples who moved from being caring and loving partners to being selfish, inconsiderate, and manipulative individuals. The words in the song include the following.

"Tell me what's wrong with you now, tell me why I never seem to make you happy though heaven knows I try. What does it take to please you? Tell me just how I can satisfy you woman, you're drivin' me wild. When I come home from workin', you're on the phone talking about how bad I treat you. Now tell me I'm wrong. You say it's me who argues, I'll say it's you. We have got to get together or baby we're through. Break up to make up, that's all we do. First you love me, then you hate me, that's a game for fools."

Marriage must be perceived as being more than a beautiful ceremony followed by an evening of glamorous dining, well-wishing toasts, and the ride into honeymoon bliss. This is no criticism of how marriage ceremonies as normally practiced. Each matrimony establishes its own form of celebration. This focus highlights marital ceremonies as a beginning process and not a defined relationship expressed. Although its true elegance is not always expressed or properly pronounced, allow me to acknowledge and emphasize that the beauty of marriage is celebrated pageantry. It is the beauty of gathering with loved ones sharing encouraging words. It is the beginning of a love relationship filled with unlimited possibilities. A marriage ceremony is all these things and more. However, the true purpose of marriage extends beyond pageantry and its celebration. It is about how to live lovingly together. Marriage includes couples growing together, learning about one another, and getting to know each other. Marriage is a sacred institution ordained by God for the purpose of combining two different lives into one love relationship. Until recent times, marriage was centered around couples making spiritual vows and committing their love before God. These ceremonial words of marital commitment included the following, "I take you to be …, to have and to hold from this day forward. For better or for worse; for richer, or for poorer, in sickness, and in health; to love and to cherish, till death do we part."

These traditional vows and words of commitment couples made to each other have at times been taken for granted. For those merely repeating words in the vows made considered these sayings as being nothing more than a wedding or ceremonial requirement. Although these words are easily spoken and soon forgotten, they nevertheless have served as the foundation for enduring commitments. Religious vows speak of God's role in the marital relationship and His requirements for having a loving family. Marriage is God's solemn commission for couples to join their lives in holy commitment to each other.

Marriages have traditionally been viewed as religious performances and an act of spiritual bonding. However, not all couples embrace this form for getting married. Therefore, couples desiring to marry without a specified religious ceremony are permitted by law to be married through civil ceremonies. Civil marriages are not a new marital process. It has always been available to couples not desiring religious-based weddings. However, due to recent federal laws granting same-sex couples the rights to receive legal marital status many couples are seeking this marital option. This is especially true for same-sex couples wanting to avoid rejections by many religious groups which refuse to accept this kind of nuptial coupling. Federal laws granting equal marital rights to all couples brought changes to marital application. This applications among many changes replaced references to man and woman and husband and wife to now read genders' identifications.

This legal pronouncement brought marital conflicts between Christian clergy whose faith, established doctrine, and religious practices forbade them to perform same sex marriages and the legal authority given to others to conduct such unions. These civil laws extended marital status to same-sex couples despite religious organizations opposing such standards. Many Christian clergies refuse to qualify such unions because same-sex marriages violate their practiced faith. The equity of civil unions is that certifying same-sex marriages can become legal by filing signed documents. Ceremonies are not necessary. This new process for marital confirmation is not limited to same-sex couples, but available to all couples not seeking traditional wedding ceremonies. Civil marriages eliminate the spiritual bonding which strengthens the required love-cords to hold couples together.

Getting married and staying married are not always mutual agreements. Couples who commit to the marriage process for any other purpose than to love, build up, and care for one another risk having a short-lived marital partnership. Spiritual or religious marriages are not guaranteed success or that couples will stay together. Couples who choose not the traditional path to ceremonial marriages are not automatically doomed to fail. Perhaps the most important concern for marriages, regardless of bonding ceremony, is God's place in the relationship. Without God's presence in marriages couples will often feel spiritually unfulfilled. Married couples who fail to honor their solemn vows and faithful commitment to each other will lack the tolerance and patience needed to stay together when experiencing difficult times. Too often they will simply give up on the relationship.

Without love being assessed to be the most powerful and important commitment couples can make, many marriages will not endure marital difficulties and struggles. That is why every married couple needs to know, understand, and become aware of the truth about a marital relationship, it is a process and not a finished product. It is developmental. Through all its imperfections, marriage connections are but a work in progress. It is not a fairy tale or mythical relationship. Even when a well-loved marriage is deemed magical. Many stories have been told of this mythical view of the marital process: boy meets girl. Girl meets boy. They fall in love. Get married. Ride off into the sunset and live happily ever after. This storybook explanation of love and marriage is not usually the way the real-life story goes. Couples who either believe this or expect this for their marriages are set up for disappointments and failures. This storybook process is not a true portrait of marital living! Real marriages do not begin with riding off into the sunset. Rather, they are more about settling down and building their lives together. Marriages provide couples opportunities to grow and develop love, peace, joy, and happiness in their relationships. Happiness is not achieved with words alone.

Marriage is a challenging relationship that often faces obstacles, and elements of division, destruction, and defeat. However, that doesn't mean or suggests that marital failures are imminent. Couples should be aware that there are enemies against marital success. These enemies exploit relationships and devise schemes purposed to destroy couples' love and commitment for one another. These enemies to marital success include infidelity, lies, deceit, adultery, and deceptive secrets. In response to these negative invaders into their marriages, couples need to refrain from using debasing or hurtful words with each other. Especially when being upset or feeling emotional. Such restraints during heated discussions or arguments should include the following, not making harmful threats, giving ultimatums, and finding faults with the marriage. Unhealthy responses will transform loving homes filled with care and respect into lonely people and empty houses. Not always intended, these kinds of engagements: hatred, resentments, and lack of trust will cost couples their homes, marriages, and good relationships. During difficult times in marriages, couples must be willing to hear what each one has to say about issues or concerns which may cause marriages to end in divorce. When couples fail to communicate about intimate concerns, they will often end the marriage with many unanswered questions. The headlined question will be, "Where did we go wrong?"

Divorce, A Last Word Spoken

Divorce is a powerful enemy which approves marriages endings. It plants bad thoughts in good relationships through deceit. It invades and uproots lasting hopes with false promises. Divorce uses pain as its major weapon to dissolve marriages wounded by betrayals. Divorce prevents marriages from becoming long-term commitments. Divorce ends marriages. It uses tools, methods, and conflicting efforts, such as unresolved issues and broken promises to accomplish its mission. For married couples to avoid this enemy's powerful imprints, they need to love their mates from their hearts which will insulate their romantic relationships from all agitators and destroyers. This unity of purpose is important for lasting love and relationships. Without this uniting love and care for each other couples' hearts may become infected with this disease known as apathy. Once apathy settles within a relationship, concern and care become byproducts of a happy marriage. Soon divorce, being cancerous to marriages, will dominate all discussions, arguments, and threats. However, when couples share genuine love, their affection will often stifle divorce's ability to invade their relationships. Divorce is too often presented as an easy way out to couples struggling through troubled relationships. During these difficult times some couples are led to believe that leaving the marriage is better than staying. They are advised to end their marriages through divorce.

If marriages are to remain valued relationships this sacred union must not be viewed by couples as temporary living arrangements. Rather, this treasured partnership must be understood as being God's designed relationship between men and women. Unfortunately, marriage as the traditional institution for established family is being upended and challenged by alternative social living conditions. Time has come for restoring marriage to again being perceived as sacred, holy, and spiritual. Alternative marriages, which permits same-sex marriages, do not have valid spiritual acceptance, regardless of what social and cultural standards accept. Far too many marriages based on secular standards and not biblical principles seem to end in divorce. For this primary reason, among many other reasons, some couples consider it to be emotionally safer to share noncommittal relationships without being married and avoid the pains of divorce rather than make a commitment to marriage and trust God for its success.

This ill-conceived philosophy for family living falsely claims that this method will avoid long-term incompatibility. It proposes to keep divorce from ever becoming an issue, consideration, or requirement. This concept of "trying it before you do it" must not be condoned as a better or acceptable standards for ensuring lasting marriages. Traditional marriages are not perfect. Their unions do not ensure that couples will be insulated from marital problems. Neither does it assure that couples would be able to avoid pains caused by divorce or its considerations. Contrary to those who want to define the marital process in their own images, the sacredness of marriages remains God's design and His plan for men and women to blend their lives into one love.

The question, 'where did we go wrong?' must be explored through the prism of making marriages work, rather than watching it become a crumbling institution of past virtues. This question offers an encouraging appeal to all marriages. Especially to troubled marriages dangling on the precipice of falling apart and heading toward destruction. However, there is hope for every troubled home, every troubled relationship, and every troubled marriage. Marriage's success is not, and will not be based on man's rationales, excuses, or alternatives. Successful marriages often are spiritually focused, and God directed. In the absences of physical abuse, psychological abuse, or mental domination by one partner over the other, couples should not seek quick ways out of their marriages. Rather, they should let patience have her perfect work. Sometimes, the flaws you see in and think about your partner, may be the same reflected flaws within yourself. If you are so quick to fall out of love with your spouse, perhaps you committed heart-fraud with pretended love when you entered the relationship. What is needed in lasting relationships is real love. Genuine love can be trusted. It is not cloaked in pretense. It grows and develops true relationships. Love does not seek reasons for separation. It strives through committed efforts to work things out. Love will not quit. It is clearly understood in spiritually formed relationships that love will keep couples and families together. "Love never gives up, never loses faith, is always hopeful, and endures through every circumstance. Love will last forever," (I Corinthians 13:7-8a, NLT). Sometimes expressed love brings a tear! Sometimes its unveiled intention invites a smile! Sometimes the reality of active love makes fantasy a weak substitute for storytelling. When love is truly expressed from heart to lips, it will be filled with and provide unending joy!

Therefore, all broken loves, hurt hearts, disappointed lovers, and marriages headed for divorce courts, please pause to consider what decisions are available to you. There are four elements of influences that often determine whether marriages will last or fails: Communication, Finances, Sex and Intimacy, and Family. These areas of support are designed to encourage marriages' success and reach their greatest potential. That is why before couples decide to divorce, they should consider and make full use of their options. Couples leaning toward getting divorced should first pursue room for reconciliation to avoid having their marriages end in some form of shame, disgrace, regrets, or rejections.

These four areas of relationship often determine marriages' ability to survive and thrive. When these areas are properly supporting marriages, they will provide homes for couples, rather than leave them living in lonely houses. Through these four categories couples will be able to discuss marital challenges and avoid the painful process of getting divorce. The question "Where did we go wrong?" should help couples discuss their differences and disconnects before deciding to end in divorce.

Although every marriage bears its own conditions, each shares a commonality. These common traits include marital struggles where couples seek to understand each other. Their past and present personal issues which may adversely affect them as a family. Also, seeking solutions to marital problems which will keep them together. If marriages are to survive couples will need to support each other during difficult times.

Marriage and divorce will be the major topic of concern and discussion throughout this reading. The lives, experiences, decisions and discussions of couples considering divorce at the expense of marital success will be explored. The challenge by couples to maintain and restore broken relationships will be explored through these marital couples: Peter and Gloria, Stan and Maria, Oliver and Sandra, George and Sandy, John and Mary who all wrestled with divorce, decided to stay together and not let go.

Therefore, if your marriage or relationship has you troubled or feeling uncertain or insecure, don't panic. Before divorce becomes the final word or causes you to throw up your hands in disgust, think it over, don't quit yet. Talk about the sparks which ignited your love, the stimulation you felt in hearing that sensitive voice on the phone. Think of all your efforts to make it work, conflicts you endured, and disappointments you have overcome. Then thoroughly examine the most important question relative to your marital relationship's survival, 'Where Did We Go Wrong?'.

Part 1

Communication
(Let's Talk About It)

Chapter 1

"Marital Relationships"

Communication is the first of the four essential marital elements which are pivotal to successful marriages. There is an old saying that goes like this, "If we don't talk, we don't communicate." Well, that's not the actual saying, but I thought it fitting for this discussion. The true saying is a biblical reference to work and responsibility, "Those unwilling to work will not get to eat" (II Thessalonians 3:10b NLT). Yet the principle can be applied to how well, clearly, and often are married couples willing to talk to each other. Without clear and understandable communication, the considered best marriages risk being interrupted or falling apart by the demons of assumptions and misinformation. Marriage is not a perfect engagement. Each marriage is confronted with its own problems and issues. These situations are as common as waking up each morning to a brand-new day. Early in marriages often couples either ignore or do not give much attention to problems which later become major conflicts. These problems are generally thought to be small, insignificant, and not requiring much concern.

Most couples realize and understand that marital living comes with personal irritations and minor to major disagreements. Through marital challenging times good, clear, and effective communication is needed to avoid inflicting greater hurt on the relationship. Clear and effective communication begins with couples sharing the same words meanings. Shared language meaning is important for better understanding of what's been said or expressed. Effective communication supports couples' efforts to keep their love alive. Without having shared words meanings, communication between married couples becomes limited in their ability to clearly express their feelings. Lack of communication will often frustrate their efforts to speak with one another and often will lead to them having conflicting conversations. Without good communication marital conversations will eventually devolve into short phrases of endearments or one-word answers. When couples lack clear communication their every problem becomes a tedious task to resolve. Little problems and unresolved issues soon escalate into greater problems and dividing issues. Eventually, without clear communication, the relationship will dissolve to the level where the only conversations that couples agree to share will be silence.

However, whenever silence is used as a method to avoid arguments, confrontations, or discussions, many issues will remain unresolved. When couples fail to speak to each other to understand what is being said, unwanted marital concerns such as suspicions, accusations, and doubts will occupy their thoughts. They will often question whether the love they share will be strong enough to last through their many troubling and misunderstanding barriers. These questions will seek answers as to what caused marriages, once filled with joy, laughter, and excitement to become dull, uninteresting, and more like being imprisoned. Each marriage provides its own answer. The one common answer could include couples' forgotten vows or broken promises of commitment. When married couples do not understand what the other is saying, they often lose interest in making efforts to have conversations. This becomes reduced personal time. Limited verbal interaction will hinder couples' moments to express or discuss their love. This lack of interactions will leave them with the perception that their words don't matter, so why waste time talking.

When married couples are experiencing unclear communication with each other, they will often find their relationships' growth hampered due to few shared conversations. Eventually because of such occurrences couples will often find themselves heading toward break-ups or divorces. Because communication is lacking among them, little problems become big issues and unresolved concerns become major contentions. Poor communication is the primary reason couples have difficult times understanding each other. If these concerns are not urgently addressed, married couples will reach declining al interests in retaining their marriages which will often dissolve into incompletion. Whenever poor communication is prevalent in marital interactions, dissatisfied couples start looking for ways to get out of their relationships, either through separation or divorce.

It is important for married couples to decide whether to separate or divorce so that they give themselves more time to get to know each other better. Usually when couples learn more about each other, likes and dislikes, their decisions provide them with changes for the better. Getting to know each other better helps couples to become more aware of what pleases his/her partner. They will learn what actions or speech may not be pleasing to him/her. They will learn what brings a smile to his/her lover's face. What irritates or causes a frown. In the relationship, each partner must be willing to listen intently to shared conversations and fully grasp what is said. Couples' efforts to learn more about themselves must be reserved in special times, specific time, and personal time for intimacy. The value of reserved time of intimacy is so that couples will be able to mold, shape, and unite their hearts together. However, without giving detailed attention to the communication process, couples' relationships may become compromised by unshared language definitions and words' misunderstandings. Couples not sharing the same words may allow expressed meanings to become marital misunderstandings and issues which bring hurt, pain, rejections and often lead to divorce. When couples' marital positions become sharp contrasts between loving unions and irreconcilable differences such changes suggest or reveal couples' inability to effectively communicate with each other. Regardless, most couples refuse to admit when their marriages fall into ill-repute that it happened because of a communication failure. Many couples convince themselves that talking to each other was never the problem, they merely disagreed all the time. Effective communication between marital couples involves the unifying process of talking, listening, speaking, hearing, understanding and being understood.

Chapter 2

Stan and Maria

Stan and Maria were from drastically different backgrounds. Stan grew up in an urban setting where he constantly fought for his survival. Maria's Hispanic heritage and culture kept her close to home and sheltered from many outside activities. Stan's experiences taught him not to trust anyone and to be extremely possessive of everything he owned. On the other hand, Maria lived in a more loving and gentle community. She was known by all to be a loving, kind, and generous person. She grew up believing that trust was a sacred value. Stan's neighborhood was often highlighted by violence. Maria's community's greatest concern was being accepted in society's mainstream. From the beginning their relationship seemed to have been an odd couple engagement. Yet they both believed that they had found their soul mate.

Their wedding was a gal affair. The ceremony was a designed combination of both cultural backgrounds. Stan's groomsmen were his neighborhood gang members. Maria's bridesmaids were her friends beautifully adorned in the colorful traditions of her Hispanic heritage. The wedding atmosphere was filled with fear and excitement. Fear from wedding guests towards the gang members attending the wedding. Excitement was for the gala celebration of the wedding ceremony by all attending guests. Regardless of the mild anxiety of the day, Stan and Maria were married. They believed that finding each other was directed by God. They believed that their marriage would last. They expected their marriage to be full of love and happiness.

However, their lives became less than what they had imagined when their contrasting backgrounds conflicted in ways which threatened their marriage. Stan became very possessive of Maria's life and was extremely jealous to the point that if any man looked at her or said anything to her, he took offense and was ready to fight. Maria's personality was polite. She had a very friendly spirit which caused most people to feel comfortable being around her. Stan often accused her of being a flirt and giving men the wrong impressions. Maria assured Stan that she was not doing anything but being polite. She did her best to affirm her devotion to him. Maria made it as plain as she could to Stan that she had no desire to seek love or affection from anyone else. Her love was for him. Him alone! Stan's jealousy wouldn't leave him convinced of Maria's devotion to him. He began monitoring her activities. Checking her cell phone to see who was calling her. He even had some of his gang members shadow her movements and report back to him. Because of his insecurity and Maria's uncertainty as to how to engage or relate to other people, their marriage soon became dull and uninviting. It shared little resemblance to the exciting and enthusiastic relationship which brought them together. Maria felt trapped in a marriage that had lost its love. Stan was frustrated that Maria couldn't understand how much love he had for her. He wanted her. He needed her. She belonged to him. Their marriage was experiencing a breakdown heading toward a breakup. Their relational dilemma became a clear example of how important it is for married couples to know one another. Couples need to learn how to get along. Couples need to know how to live together.

Why is communication a hard thing to establish and achieve in marriages? Among many reasons are those which include, like other people, couples who think that talking is communicating. Talking is the basic mode of humans' verbal expressions. However, talking is not always communicating. Couples which fail to speak with the same words meaning, understanding of, and shared definitions will continue to take past each other. The failure to communicate is a major reason why marital relationships often decline. There is a fair contrast in knowing the difference between talking and communicating. Talking is about words made into sentences to convey a specific thought or reference. Communication is the process of understanding words spoken with agreed meaning and understanding.

Talking among people is commonly accepted as communicating. Therefore, many married couples convinced themselves that because they talk, they know what their partners are saying or intend to say. However, without having a shared communication language, one partner's expressed message may be completely opposite in meaning to the other partner's understanding. Stan and Maria communication failures were not limited to what verbal languages they used, but the nonverbals were also major obstacles for them. Maria's hand gestures helped her express her thoughts, ideas, and intimate desires. Stan often misunderstood them and assumed she was either pointing fingers at him or wanting to slap him. Whenever she turned away from him during discussions, he felt that she didn't value his opinions or respected his sayings. However, for Maria, Stan's violent temper always thrusted her into panic and fear that his physical gestures would one day hurt her. Although neither one of them meant any harm or danger to the other, their undefined animated expressions and lack of shared language understanding left them with their own meanings and conclusions.

Chapter 3

A Shared Love Language

Language is a fragile method of expression used by humans when it comes to thoughts, feelings, and ideas. Language is a clumsy means by which information sharing takes place. Language is diverse in meanings and more complex in its applications. Nevertheless, language is the necessary tool given to us by which communication and conversations may occur. Language, shared language, is the pathway to understanding. It provides directions and confirms life's purposes. Spoken language is essential to the communication process, even at times when it is conveyed awkwardly or incoherently. Therefore, couples must diligently pursue understanding of their partners' thoughts, responses, and word-language. Without understanding many marital problems are found embedded in confusion. Often relationship problems result in couples becoming negative towards each other and engaging in name calling. Unkind and demoralizing statements focused on being humiliating will become the war tool couples will use for battle. These kinds of problems include conflicts and insensitive comments which at the end yield themselves to pain, suffering, unhappiness, criticism, and blame. The more negatives' couples hurl at each other, the more they will tear down what they were trying to build up.

Wisdom for resolving many marital disputes and arguments which may lead to separations can be reaped from the pen of King Solomon who is often credited with being the wisest man ever to live. "Live happily with the woman you love through all the meaningless days of life that God has given you in this world. The wife God gives you is your reward for all your earthly toil," (Ecclesiastes 9:9, NLT).

During courtships couples rarely spend time dissecting each other's communication skills. They merely ignore words, sayings, and expressions they don't know or identify with as being a big deal. Even when things said may be awkward or uncomfortable they pretend that such sayings have no effect on them. They are emotionally bonded. Each absent moment from the other forces anxious interest of longings, and 'can't wait to see you' desires. For the most part their courtship, which placed stars in their eyes, songs in their hearts, was later discovered to have been nothing more than a mythical love. Those elevated feelings gave them reasons to love and fall in-love. A love which at times was filled with bursting enthusiasm and excitement. Although these couples were sharing times and memorable moments together, it was assumed they were communicating. Many things said, during those times, may not have been clearly spoken and easily understood. Nevertheless, for couples experiencing this stage of romantic interactions, little differences mattered because for them, love was in the air. Love was all that they needed. Whatever speech, talk, or words spoken, regardless of how well, poorly, clearly, or cloudy presented, was not important, significant, or of great concerns. Being in love and being with that special loved one was all that mattered.

The process for saving marriages heading toward divorce requires couples to be willing to examine and define their understanding of marriage. Does their concept of marriage include a willingness to make personal sacrifices and needed compromises? Do they value understanding as the most essential element in the relationship relative to facing conflicts or challenges? Do their understanding of marriage prevent them from allowing issues to cause their shared relationship to decline making divorce a topic of discussions? Will their partnership marriage keep them reminded of their love, even through difficult times?

Shared marital perspectives will provide couples reasons to stay together. It will preserve what they have built together. It will prevent couples from concluding that marital life has lost its luster, personal and sexual appeal. It's the depth of love which makes marriage significant. Did they understand that building a married life together involved struggles, challenges, arguments, and disagreements? Was marriage always a deep-rooted expectation for bonded relationships or merely an ideal consideration or sentimental journey? According to the Gospel of Saint Mark 10:6-9 (NLT), "But God's plan was seen from the beginning of creation, for 'He made them male and female.' This explains why a man leaves his father and mother and is joined to his wife, and the two are united into one. Since they are no longer two but one, let no one separate them, for God has joined them together."

Couples who are determined not to have their marriages end in divorce must focus on shared love. They should give each other their loving attention and avoid creating marital conflicts through arguments and separation discussions. Couples' attraction to each other can basically be mounted on one of two foundational emphases. One is physical, and the other is spiritual attractions. Physical remains the primary attraction of this foundational position which focuses on outside appearances. There is an adage that goes along with this perspective, 'you can't judge a book by its cover.' Additionally, to this attention toward how people look is the shallow attraction to fame, fortune, and lustful desires. Spiritual attraction, which is the second foundational position, focuses on peoples' hearts, personalities, and personal attitudes. These elements give relationships their greater sense of purpose, meaning, and understanding of love's great value. Couples which apply spiritual principles in their love relationships will make deliberate efforts to keep God in their marriages. Although each attraction has inherited faults, disappointments, and even failures, between the two options, spiritual attractions provide couples with the greater marital opportunity for success. The spiritual principles of marital engagements are foundationally grounded in understanding, commitment, and recognition that marriage is a sacred love institution. Marriage was established by God and designed for building lasting love relationships.

"Therefore, shall a man leave his father and his mother, and shall cleave unto his wife, and they shall be one flesh," (Genesis 2:24, KJV). The Bible further emphasizes marital sanctity this way, "Marriage is honourable in all, and the bed undefiled," (Hebrews 13:4a, KJV). Christians believe that marriage is a sacred agreement between man and woman to love and care for each other 'til death do they part.' Christian weddings usually find couples making vows of commitment to each other. They are charged by the clergy to be sure of the lifelong commitment they are making. They are reminded that marriages should not be entered into hurriedly, anxiously, or without consideration of the requirements. Marriage is not to be carelessly sought or lightly engaged.

Rhythm and blues singer Percy Sledge, in his 1968 song entitled, "Take Time to Know Her," tells of the negative consequences and discouraging results when anxious couples get married before getting to know one another. In this song, a good simple-minded man meets a woman in which he immediately falls in love with and wants to marry her. He doesn't know anything about her life, her lifestyle, her background information, or her personal interests. He's not concerned with any of those inquiries. He only wants her. He sees her only in the lights of his attraction to her being the woman of his dream. He is so excited about her that he couldn't wait to have her meet his mother. When his mother meets her, she makes no judgments, but quietly advises her son to take time to know her. She tells him not to rush into marriage. Well, the son did not heed his mother's advice. He hurriedly married this woman because he was so in love with her. Although the preacher who performed the ceremony cautioned him to take time to know her and not to rush into this thing. He did not heed the warning from these two people in his life. However, after he and the woman were married, he came home early one day from work and found his wife with another man. Heartbroken, and discouraged, he remembered his mother's advice, "Son, take time to know her. It's not an overnight thing. Take time to get to know her. Please don't rush into this thing." Couples who hurry into marriages without giving themselves time to process the commitment being made often leave themselves vulnerable to misunderstanding, disappointments, bitterness, and anger. These negative emotions usually prompt struggling couples to reach the conclusion that the only way to end the hurts they have experienced is through divorce.

From the beginning marriages were intended to be life-long commitments between men and women. Divorce was not to be an associated consideration with marriage. During Jesus ministry days he was confronted with the question of divorce by religious leaders seeking to trap and accuse Him of breaking the law. Jesus met their challenges with the acknowledgement that divorce was not God's design for marriages. However, through Moses' teachings they were permitted to write a bill of divorce. At this time only the men were given the authority to initiate the divorce process. Jesus explained why this was permitted. "For the hardness of your heart he wrote you this precept. But from the beginning of the creation God made them male and female. For this cause shall a man leave his father and mother and cleave to his wife; And they twain shall be one flesh: So, then they are no more twain, but one flesh.

What therefore God hath joined together, let no man put asunder," (Mark 10:5-9, KJV).

This marital permission became an abusive method by which men, not women, had the authority to end their marriages without any specific reasonings. This process put women at great disadvantages. They had no voice in the process. Jesus addressing this subject said, "Whosoever shall put away his wife, let him give her a writing of divorcement. But I say unto you, that whosoever shall put away his wife, saving for the cause of fornication, causeth her to commit adultery: and whosoever shall marry her that is divorced committed adultery," (Matthew 5:31-32, KJV).

Perhaps this might have been the condition under which the historical Samaritan woman of the Bible found herself. She is commonly referred to as being the 'Woman at The Well.' Her story included the pronounced assertion that she had been married five times (and divorced that number of times) and the man she lived with was not her husband (John 4:1-18, KJV). This woman having been married and divorced these many times she was often talked about and ridiculed. The criticism of her was so severe and personally debasing that she didn't enjoy the company, friendship, fellowship, and other personal interactions with the women of her town. Most people reading and discussing her story lay the blame at her feet, but what if she had no voice in the matter? Because Samaritans followed the same religious practices as the Jews, she was probably the victim in each of the divorced relationships as would be the Jewish wives. Remember, when the man wanted to remove a woman from the marriage all he had to do was write her a bill of divorcement, and the marriage was over (Matthew 5:31, KJV). This Samaritan woman who was coming to the well for her daily supply of water had no voice, no standings, and no rights to change her status or condition. Her livelihood was under the care of the man. Her welfare was at the mercy of her husband. She could perhaps have been more aptly presented as being a prisoner of an unfair culture rather than a woman of ill-repute.

Marriage is a shared partnership which gives neither person any control advantages over the other. When one person in the marriage attempts to dictate or dominate how the marriage will be conducted, that relationship will lose its ability to accept love. Although such couples may remain together in their marriages, the love, cohesion, and shared intimacy of the relationship will be empty and void of feelings. Effective communication, wholesome discussions, and heart-felt talks will prevent the need for either partner to assume power, authority, or control in the relationship. Love will prompt all their actions, secure their personal esteem, speak to their intimate needs, deal with sensitive issues, work through difficult problems, and hold them firmly together. Marriages which merge two lives into one love begin with shared words and expressions communicated from the heart. Couples which struggle to understand each other's languages will often find it difficult to communicate. Time will be spent hearing words spoken, yet their talking will never bridge the gap which exists between communication and understanding. Therefore, couples lacking essential merging communication elements will often find their marital relationship filled with frustration, unresolved issues, and unhappy living.

"Security of Love"

Peter and Gloria spent much time talking about issues which troubled their marriage. Their conversations often had more disagreements than agreements. They soon realized that their poor communication was damaging their home, their lives, and the love they valued. To preserve their love relationship, they found it essential for them to listen more intently during their conversations. It had been during their conversations that they spent time talking over rather than to one another. Their level of communication was so poor that they often dreaded having conversations for fear that their relationship would further decline. Therefore, there were many conversations they avoided talking about with each other. During a few of their intimate talks they learned that it was important for them to accept and value what each one had to say. This understanding of valuing each other restored the joy they desired for their marriage.

Peter and Gloria learned that marriage and personal appreciation come through shared ideas, shared thoughts, and better understanding. It became effectively important for them to know how to lovingly speak to each other and express their heart-felt intentions. They, with desire to maintain peace and harmony in their marriage, avoided making concerned issues divisive or negative during discussions.

During their courtship, Peter and Gloria didn't spend time learning much about each other. Therefore, like many newly married couples, they struggled in their relationship to know and understand one another. Realizing their failure in this department of their relationship, they made personal efforts to work together so that they could live together. They soon learned that similar backgrounds did not guarantee shared virtues and same values. Their different life paths and backgrounds had exposed and conditioned them to different ways of living. Although there were some distinct differences between their approach to living and marriage, they like other newlywed couples, initially thought that their backgrounds differences would not make such difference. However, they would soon discover that unaddressed background differences often lead to unintentional marital conflicts, problems, and troubles.

Marriage is not a finished product. During its process, two lives are blended into one sacred bond of love and commitment. This marital process involves Shared differences which allows differing expressions of topics, issues, various activities, and events to occur. Discussions of some past topics require courage to share or provide detailed information. The reason why married couples sharing their past may require courage to do so is that some shared information could be difficult to handle or accept. Peter and Gloria met at a time when they both felt betrayed and abandoned by their lovers. Their shared history was about pain, hurts, disappointments, and loss. Yet they had the courage to talk about it and to share its impact on how they lived. However, not all married couples possess this kind of courage. Sometimes sharing one's history may jeopardize how he/she is perceived or understood. Some marital partners may assume that certain past behaviors were unacceptable acts and used them against him/her as personal shortcomings. That is why honesty is the best way to avoid being tagged with unjust labeling, negative thoughts, or feelings of being trapped in these differences. Because small irritating things will soon develop into aggravations which cause friction in the marriage. Honest expressions of feelings and thoughts between couples will help them to find better grounds for agreements and acceptance.

Little irritating things can become major causes of dissensions in marriages. Therefore, small things, things thought to be small, and insignificant things can create great problems in marital relationships. For example, such small things as how toothpaste is squeezed from the tube could become an irritation (one squeezes from the top, the other squeezes from the bottom or middle). The toilet paper in the bathroom may be an argued item (rolling the paper from the top or rolling it from the bottom). These are little things until there are many of them. Alone, they don't seem to matter much. Alone, they are just individual irritations. Not real agitational concerns. However, together they are a mess.

Peter and Gloria allowed such small irritations in their relationship to become major reasons for them to find faults and to become aggravated with each other. The main issue in this fault-finding saga was Peter and Gloria inability to share serious conversations about their problems. They constantly talked around issues which were hurting their marriage. They lacked marital courage to directly address them. They were not willing to confront their problems through honest dialogues and shared conversations. They became discouraged from attempting to confront and discuss their marital problems. Soon they were aware that communication was their major problem. They made deliberate efforts to share and understand their thoughts and opinions. They agreed to listen more attentively to what was being said. They also agreed to make sure that what was heard was the intended message. They realized that they had problems with discussing marital issues. They learned from each other during this getting-to-know process that failure to establish good communication leads to misunderstanding, misinterpretation, and brokenness. However, when couples share the same meanings of words, same definitions of words, and have understanding between them, they avoid many conflicts.

Chapter 4

"Don't Take Flowers Off the Table"

Peter and Gloria's wedding ceremony was simply pageantry fit for royalty. It was filled with romance and beauty. The setting was picturesque. The atmosphere was joyous. This day had all the inklings of a loving relationship reflecting a lasting happy marriage. When the ceremony was completed, this newly bonded couple rode off in a limousine to experience their honeymoon bliss. The pleasure they found in each other's arms heightened their expectations of building a home where they would grow old together. At first, nothing they did or encountered robbed them of the joy and excitement they found in each other. Constantly being in each other's presence made them feel complete. They laughed. They talked. They held hands outside, walking in the park, going up and down the stairwells. Happiness personified their marriage.

Unfortunately, the love shared in their relationship blinded them to the reality of living after the ceremony and managing marital concerns. After a few months of amorous delights, they found their relationship plagued with marital issues which challenged their marriage ability to last. They learned that marital issues must be discussed before they become negative influences and rob the marriage of its joyful bliss. This will gradually change the home atmosphere. Little things, once ignored, will begin to irritate. For example, Peter had a bad habit of coming home from work leaving his dirty shoes in the middle of the sitting room. The irritating thing for Gloria about this seemingly innocent habit was that they would leave noticeable shoe marks on the floor. Floors which she spent hours cleaning. His dirty shoes came from his job and walking through construction sites. He was the city's building inspector. As financially rewarding his job was for the family, his habit of leaving his dirty shoes in the wrong places became an unacceptable irritant for Gloria. Although Peter's inconsideration bothered Gloria, she was not without her acts of irritation to Peter. Gloria worked at the local high school as an educational counselor. She was a perfectionist when it came to being clean. Each day after school she would spend extra hours cleaning her work area, and the same when she was home. She wanted her home to be both as clean and spotless as possible.

Having grown up in an environment where trash, garbage, and other debris were common eyesores, she was determined to never live in such conditions again. For Gloria, dirt, trash, or other debris were not to be found or reside in her house. Therefore, living under these restraints in his home became an intolerable and uneased conditions for Peter. He was not close to being concerned with cleanliness as was Gloria. In fact, he was a little sloppy. Early in their marriage Gloria tried to ignore this annoyance, but it grated on her sense of comfort. She tried politely to let Peter know that she preferred him not to bring his dirty shoes into the house. Not realizing the depth of what was being said, Peter smiled and said that he would try to do better. He never considered this to be a major issue or anything worth giving a second thought. He was wrong! This was a major topic which needed his first-class attention. Without thinking or being aware of the depth of consternation his actions or inactions caused Gloria, he continued leaving his shoes in the middle of the sitting room. Gloria felt that Peter's seeming lack of respect for her request to maintain a clean house was very disrespectful. Gloria felt uncomfortable and saddened that she was forced to live in a filthy setting. Gloria felt that she was unappreciated, disrespected, dejected, and that Peter didn't care about her feelings.

On the other side of the proverbial coin, Peter had a few objections of his own about Gloria's obsession with cleanliness. It irritated him that she possessed this 'everything must be clean' attitude. It irritated him that she would constantly ignore his needs by spending what seemed like hours cleaning the bathroom, taking a bath, or redecorating the items in either the bedroom, living room, and/ or dining room. It irritated him that whenever it came to planning family events, it was always her way or no way. Regardless to what he offered, she always cancelled out his suggestions. Talking about being comfortable in his own home! No way! She constantly made him feel like the house they were supposed to be making into a home was more like a showroom or a display house. He didn't say much about his discomfort with the way he felt forced to live because she seemed happy and satisfied. However, Peter felt sad because he was unable to please his wife. He came to believe that Gloria only paid attention when he did negative things. She made him feel like he was to her nothing but a 'messy lost cause.' He built up silent resentments toward Gloria. The silent resentments they each carried in their hearts developed into negatives thoughts about each other. As a result of their silent objections their relationship became more about criticisms, critiques, fault-findings, and negative comments. Gloria's negative assessments of Peter, considering their declining marital conditions, caused her to second guess herself about her choice of men. She chastised herself asking how could she have been attracted to such a dirty inconsiderate person as the man who became her husband? Peter's opinion about their declining marriage had him dreading coming home at the end of his workday. He began welcoming the lights of a new day. Each morning signaled a new day which gave him reason and permission to get away from the house.

Peter and Gloria's marriage slowly and steadily moved away from being the loving relationship envisioned it would be. This once happy and joyous couple now found less joy in spending time together. They allowed minor conflicts to become major problems in their marriage because they were unwilling to talk about issues to each other. Instead of sharing their honest feelings, they talked around what they needed to express or make known. In conversations they spoke politely, but not with the same loving passion which attracted them to each other. The air of dissension between them became so thick that often silence became their best mode of conversation. Knowing that pretense has a short lifespan, one day their silence erupted into a volcano of unsavory words which destroyed the peaceful acceptance of their unspoken misery. Bitter words, hurtful words spewed from their lips. Words which should have been spoken with the purpose of seeking understanding instead sputtered viciously from their mouths or perhaps more honestly from their hearts. Gloria speaking to Peter said, "You are a dirty filthy person with the brain of a pig. I must've been blind not to see what I was getting into." Peter responding to Gloria's insult was equally cruel. "You are an intolerable woman who makes living with you both a misery and a pain of which no man should be required to endure." Gloria, not to be out insulted, shouted back, "What makes you think living with a person who has an IQ of a mentally retarded bat would have an appreciation for a cultured woman as me?" Peter, in an angry threatening deep striking tone, retorted "I am so tired of walking around you like I'm treading eggshells." (He picked up the vase of beautifully decorated flowers serving as the dining room table's centerpiece). "I feel like tossing this vase against the walls and watch it splatter everywhere." Gloria recognized how out of control their argument or confrontation had become thought to soften the atmosphere. "Please don't take the flowers off the table," she quietly requested. "They are not the reason we are hurting one another." Not to be outdone, Peter softened his tone as well and became more considerate of what was occurring. He realized that it would be in his best interest to appear as civil as Gloria during this dispute so no blame for their marital failure would fall on him. "What has become of us?" He asked. "Where has the love gone?" "I thought that you said you loved me." He points at Gloria and asks her,

"What can I say to you to make things better or right?" Gloria paused for a moment and in a cold-hearted tone "Nothing! We are done! I want a divorce."

What happened to this couple? Where was the breakdown in their relationship? The answer was always in front of them. Their talks were not enough to sustain them. They failed to communicate the love needed to keep them together. They were only left with the question, Where Did We Go Wrong?

Chapter 5

"Coordinated Romance Or Not!"

Oliver and Sandra grew up in the same neighborhood, went to the same high school, and for a short period of time were known to be in a very serious intimate love relationship. As a couple, they seemed a natural fit and destined to be together forever. The adoring affections they had for one another and the detailed attention they gave each other was displayed as a model of true love. Their every action and involvement complemented the love they shared. It appeared to all who knew, observed, and watched them grow closer together that they shared an inseparable kind of love. However, after graduating from high school they decided to trust the security of their love by attending colleges in different states. This separation became a trust test of their love. It challenged their love which caused them to face the difficult obstacles of staying together while being apart. At first it appeared that their agreed plan for staying connected during their separation didn't pose any relationship problems. Initially, Oliver and Sandra stayed true to their agreement to maintain a commitment to love and keep their weekend rendezvous. Throughout the week they kept in contact through phone conversations. Everything was lining up as they had projected to keep their love alive.

However, as with all long distant relationships, not only do locations separate people, but also time. As time passed this loving couple noticed the impact of being separated. Their lives took on new interests. They met and made new friends whose influences caused changes in their goals, motivations, and people in their lives. Laura was a beautiful young girl among Oliver's new friends. Her influence on him became so strong that he soon forgot his commitment to Sandra. Laura's deceptive love stole Oliver's affections and moments of intimacy previously reserved for Sandra. This opening for someone to interrupt his relationship with Sandra was there because maintaining a long-distance love connection is always difficult to do. They found it difficult to maintain the relationship. They each needed someone to fill their personal attention gap which this distant romance could not fill. New people. New changes. Oliver and Sandra became in each other's eyes different people from whom they had known. They had become a distant couple. They once shared a love so deep that it was believed would last forever. Now having been separated from that love, they were faced with options of establishing new lives, new friends, and new love interests. Oliver and Sandra realized that for them to continue pretending that their distant love could be maintained would only invite one or both to stray from their agreement and commitment. Therefore, the once relished love relationship began to decline with fewer calls made, infrequent contacts occurred, and excuses constantly given for missed planned occasions. After all these activities piled up, they agreed to end the relationship, but to remain friends.

Agreeing to remain friends seemed like the noble and amicable way to end the relationship without appearing no longer caring! Perhaps! Regardless! The love that once captured their hearts was no longer available for them. Time and distance changed their focus, interest, and intimate moments. Their once reserved times for shared love had been stolen and replaced with new people in their lives. This eventually caused the relationship to end. Their new lives, new people, and new interests took each of them on journeys different from the roads they had sought to travel together.

Oliver married Laura, his college girlfriend. Their marriage lasted five years. The marital relationship between Oliver and Laura was years filled with dissension and mistrust. Among the missing elements lacking in this marriage was a loving relationship focused on heart-felt intimacy. Although Oliver worked hard to make their marriage work, Laura soon became tired of him. All the things they seemed to have in common while dating was later found to be a courtship façade. After being married for a few years, Oliver found his heart broken over a love that didn't last, and a true love he left behind. It happened this way. One afternoon he came home from work to find out that his wife had checked out of the relationship. She left him a small note which read, "I'm gone!" Oliver realized that running after her would not bring him either joy or satisfaction filed for and was granted a divorce from Laura.

On the other side of this story of love, regret, and renewal, Sandra became involved with one of her college professors who had recently become a widower. He lost his wife to cancer. His marriage to Sarah, his deceased wife, was a treasured 30-year long romance. After her death the Professor found himself to be quite lonely and in desperate need of a woman to share his love. When Sandra showed interest in sharing time with him, he felt renewed in spirit. Also, he being an elderly man was flattered that a beautiful young woman like Sandra wanted to be with him. He was not aware that Sandra too was lonely and searching for someone who would love her. Soon this May to December relationship was consummated in marriage. However, their union came under scrutiny from outside people who were willing to judge Sandra as a gold-digger kind of a woman. Those who sat in such judgment didn't know her. They were wrong about her. She was not looking for a sugar daddy relationship. She wanted to love and be loved.

Perhaps it was the Professor's loving and caring approach to her which made him seem special. Maybe it was his regal glow which attracted her to him. Regardless, the Professor's kind and respectful manners toward her gave Sandra the assurance and comfort she needed to trust him, loving her. They became involved. Their marriage was truly a May to December romance. Unfortunately for Sandra and the Professor, their marriage was short-lived. The Professor became ill and died. He was diagnosed with the same terminal cancer as Sarah, his deceased wife. Without their knowledge they had been exposed indirectly to some chemical toxins which caused them to develop lung cancer. Sandra, not knowing about this aspect of his health, showered him with love, attention, and care which he had not experienced since Sarah died. Complementary to his gentlemen characteristics, the Professor treated Sandra like the princess she desired to be adored. Then it happened. His time came to an end. The Professor on his death bed took Sandra by her hand and held it securely in his hands. He pulled her closer to him. Kissed her hand and whispered endearing words of love for her to remember, "You are my forever princess!" He then closed his eyes and slept away. Sandra was heartbroken for the loss of this precious man in her life. However, she was grateful that God gave her this man to love.

The lives of Oliver and Sandra had decisively taken sharp turns from the life they had planned together. Starting over in the game of love was an uncomfortable process for them. Oliver became disheartened and disappointed because of how sudden his marriage to Laura ended. He became unsure as to whether it was worthwhile for him to pursue love again. Before his marriage to Laura ended in divorce and disappointment, Oliver thought that people got married to live happily together. He thought that all that a man needed for him to have a successful marriage was a tenderhearted woman to love and call his own. An honest woman who had a loving devotion for him. A good woman who would be committed to making marriage a lasting relationship. Contrarily, Oliver's collapsed marriage to Laura, his college girlfriend, left his spirit wounded and his heart deeply scarred. Their broken relationship left him hurting from the stings and pains of marital rejection, failure, and incompletion.

Sandra, having been cast aside by Oliver for another woman, decided to move on with her life. She felt crushed because the love she treasured was stolen from her. She didn't see it coming. Although she should have noticed the signs indicating that his attitude and commitment toward her were changing. His actions and times with her were being challenged by new interests and influences in his life. Soon it became obvious to Sandra, their relationship was over. Sandra was left with only memories of what they shared as a couple. These memories often caused her to become depressed when she thought of them as she tried to understand what went wrong. Their relationship seemed so perfect to her. He loved her and she loved him. They had each other. Now it was gone. Distant love caused Oliver's attention to seek pleasures in another woman's arms. She was left alone.

Efforts to avoid her empty feelings and loneliness, Sandra made herself available as a volunteer in the Community Center. She took delight in helping people who often came into the Center with a myriad of issues and problems. Sometimes she would sit and listen to lonely people whose only need was to have someone hear their pains. Often, she found herself dismissing her own struggles with loneliness to give them her undivided attention. Unknowing to her, the kindness and care in which she engaged others, would be the magnet which caused her to meet a kind and gentle man who wanted her for himself. As if it was a storybook setting, Sandra was swept off her feet by this elderly man who being enamored with her beauty gave her all the attention she desired. The Professor, as she came to know him, recognized that the beauty in this woman was displayed in her personality and her for care for others. The Professor thought that Sandra giving her precious time, attention, and concerns for other people made her an extraordinary person. Sandra's unselfishness so fascinated the Professor that he wanted to do special things for her so that she would know that others appreciated her kindness. He wanted her to know that she was loved. He believed that it was time that Sandra received the same kind of love she often gave others. Therefore, in the presence of many, he bowed on one knee and asked her to marry him.

From the start of this storybook romance until the day he closed his eyes in death, the Professor did his best to elevate Sandra's belief in herself and her self-esteem. He made great efforts to let her know that he loved her and would always recognize her as his beautiful queen. He delighted in giving her any and everything her heart desired. His primary motivation was to make her happy. Often, he told her that God had blessed him to have two wives who were distinct, unique, and extraordinarily beautiful women. Not at any time did he violate his love and devotion with either one. His first wife Sarah became ill and died suddenly leaving him lonely and in need of tender loving companionship. Being an elderly man, he dared not trust his own instincts. Instead, he prayed and asked

God for such a person to wipe away his loneliness and to give him someone that he could love. Someone who would not take advantage of his love. He believed Sandra to be God's gift to him.

The Professor died after living a few happy years with Sandra. According to the Professor, Sandra's love took away his emptiness and restored the joy of living to him. After his death Sandra once again found loneliness to be her companion. Many men tried to capture her attention and affection, but her husband had set such high standards for showering her with love, care, and special attention that it was difficult for any of them to qualify or capture it. Life became difficult for Sandra to find purpose and meaning. Days became more like weeks, weeks more like months, and months more like years. Sad times. Sandra tried desperately to replace her loss of companionship with events and activities. Nothing seemed capable of measuring up to the standards and joyful life she enjoyed with the Professor.

It was a hot summer day when Sandra returned home for her 20th high school class reunion. Feeling a little reluctant about seeing some classmates after all these years, she thought the reunion would provide a few moments of delight. She needed something to fill the void in her life. After going back and forth in her thinking about attending the reunion, she wondered what the social decorum would be. Would it be more like being with a bunch of playful overgrown juveniles, or in a parade, or an evening of listening to overachievers bragging and modeling their success to impress others? She wondered whether it would even be beneficial for her to attend. She reasoned with herself that not going would mean nothing lost because after all this time who would she remember? Who would remember her? She barely remembered any of their names. However, knowing how life changes people's appearances, she doubted whether she would recognize anyone. Nevertheless, she motivated herself to give this event a try and do her best to get through it.

Then this unsuspecting moment happened. She noticed a person standing alone. She wondered whether he was alone or waiting for someone. She slowly moved into the ballroom surprised to find the setting so warm and welcoming. It felt good to her to be at her class reunion. Although she didn't recognize anyone, nor did anyone seem to recognize her. Immediately after finding an isolated seat to observe the many former classmates attending the event, still this isolated man was standing alone. Coming closer to where he was standing, she recognized him to be Oliver, the past love of her life. He was the one person in her class which she knew very well. Although many years had come and gone between them, she was glad to see him. They talked and talked and talked! Reliving old memories. They soon found themselves in each other's arms reliving the love they left behind. It appeared that life's circle had brought them back together. Their natural romance took them faster than perhaps their lives should have moved. Before long, they were planning a wedding that would leapfrog over past years and connect them back to the times they shared together.

Oliver and Sandra were happy being together again. Was it fate? Providence? Or by-chance? Whichever one it was it didn't matter to them. They were back into each other's arms again. They were together again! Because of the consequences of their past marriages, they were free to engage in the love that brought back meaning to their past. There weren't any obstacles which prevented them from picking up from where they had distanced them-selves. However, they would soon learn that like in most cases, their yesterdays were meant to remain yesterday. Today is life now. When couples like Oliver and Sandra try starting again a relationship which ended with hurt, pain, and disappointment, they must not only consider the impact of their breakup, but they must also be willing to let go of yesterday's troubles. They must allow now be who they are now.

Oliver and Sandra got married again! This time to each other. However, unlike before when they were with-out prior relational commitments, this time they were bringing into the marriage personal experiences and marital histories. Oliver and Sandra believed what they learned from previous marriages would provide them with a better understanding of married life. They each had developed their likes and dislikes about partnership living. Often, when couples live their marriages or relationships on feelings alone their partnerships end in disappointments. Successful loving relationships must possess the intended efforts to move past yesterday's failures in pursuit of better tomorrows. In other words, stop looking back, go forward.

Oliver and Sandra's previous marriages were supposed to have been a new beginning of love for each of them. However, it seemed that soon as their marriages began, they ended abruptly. Oliver's ended in divorce. Death was the reason Sandra's ended. Now, having found each other again, they thought it necessary to evaluate married life through their previous experiences. They thought it necessary to discuss what they thought would make marriage a lasting partnership or what would cause it to fail. Some relational elements they agreed would make the difference included love, tenderness, trust, and appreciation. They further agreed that a marriage lacking these personal traits would dissolve into routine interactions. Instead of them sharing hugs with confirmed love, they settle for heartless and empty embraces. Instead of speaking and hearing tender caring words of love and desire, their conversations become impassionate words.

Oliver and Sandra's rekindled relationship and second attempt at marriage was an opportunity for them to make their initial partnership dream a reality. Yet, they weren't quite convinced that this opportunity was real. They weren't sure whether their 'begin again' relationship had occurred out of sympathy, convenience, or a well-timed renewal. In either consideration, they didn't think either aspect was a working solution for a long-term marriage. Nevertheless, they went ahead with the marriage, bypassing all the questions and doubts they were thinking. There was a fear surrounding their renewed relationship. A shared fear of losing one another again. A shared fear of being blamed if the marriage didn't work out. A shared fear that their relationship would be determined a failure.

The joy of their marriage was short-lived. After living together for a while their adjustment problems revealed potential differences which caused them concerns. Although they shared a history, because of separation and other relationships, they needed to learn about each other again. They needed time, personal time, intimate time to know more about their expected lifetime partnership. However, conflicts occurred which interrupted the process they needed to get close to each other. One such conflict was their work schedules. Oliver's work schedule had him getting home around midnight. Sandra's business required her to start very early in the morning hours.

Their untimely schedules gave them little time together. This became a major problem in that they were unable to consistently initiate sexual and intimate times.

Oliver, being inconsiderate of Sandra's early work schedule, became agitated with her because she was going to bed before he got home. This prevented him from having sex with her. Sandra felt that Oliver was insensitive to her need for rest, knowing that he came home late, and she had to get up early. This marital obstacle caused deep resentment in their relationship. Recognizing the importance for them to resolve this issue, they agreed to work out a schedule for coordinated intimate and romantic times. Their plan initially seemed good and logical. However, it became a disaster. Their coordinated sexual times lacked intimacy and soon became stale, robotic, and less satisfying than before they tried this type of interactions. They both felt unfulfilled in their bedroom engagements. Therefore, they agreed that their relationship was not working as they had desired it to do. So instead of living this charade marriage, they decided to call it quits. They were baffled that their renewed relationship did not work. They assumed that despite their times apart, fate brought them together again. Although they believed their union to be spiritually inspired, they realized that it would be best for them if they simply walked away to find happiness with someone else. They didn't have an answer to the question, where did we go wrong?

Chapter 6

"The Way People Think"

Married couples do not begin their relationships free of predetermined thoughts, ideas, or expectations. More often they already have formed views of themselves, life itself, and the world order. All activities done in the relationship are influenced by what each person has been taught, learned, opined, and experienced. All elements of couples' living play significant roles in the marriage process. These articles of life will affect the shape, growth, and sustainability of relationships involved. The way each person thinks will give evidence to the actions performed in the relationship.

Thinking is a cog in the wheel of the communication process. Many people in relationships are baffled that their discussions on marital issues sometimes become frustrating because their words are misunderstood or misapplied.

The problem in such interactions is that couples often assume that spoken words are their only communication tool. Although words are readily recognized and accepted as a major part of the messaging process, communication is not limited to words only. The process also includes gestures and various other expressions.

In the communication circle, men and women often differ in their thoughts and observation patterns. Men are perceived to be more big-picture focused. Women are more detailed directed. Unless couples understand how information is processed by his/her partner, communication in the relationship will continue to be an unreachable agreement. Another pattern differences between the two is that men are usually less verbal or do less talking during shared conversations. Women are more inclined to be more conversational and speak openly about their feelings and concerns. These differences sometime cause contentious conflicts between couples when women interpret their men not saying much to mean that they are not concerned. Perhaps to conclude that men are less involved and not willing to deal with marital issues because of their silence could be erroneous. When there is a communication gap between couples many things said and done could be wrongly interpreted. Therefore, when marital discussions become heated arguments, things are said which maybe should not be said because one or both could be adversely hurt. The last thing couples need or should want is for either one after an argument to be left feeling put down, taken for granted, or unimportant.

Couples desiring to keep and strengthen their marriages must be aware that their relationships cannot rely on physical connections only. There must be room for spiritual engagements. Especially marriages which began with sacred vows and spiritual commitments by couples to stay together. When temptations come to end the relationship because of marital difficulties, keeping things together is often more than couples can achieve alone. Having God residing in marital relationships provides couples the energy required for them to work together and stay together. This spiritual resolve encourages struggling couples to keep their faith in God. Especially when strains of martial living challenge their will to stay together. God's solutions for troubled and challenged marriages will change things. It will turn potential break-ups into love-worthy make-up. Couples desiring to mend broken pieces in their relationships will find strong recovery power when they allow 'just a little talk with Jesus' to be inserted into their discussions. When couples use the traditional marriage ceremony to join their lives together, they invoke God's name and make marital and spiritual commitments before Him. They vow to not allow anything or anyone to separate or divide them.

Marriage, created by God, was instituted as a spiritual method of connecting man and woman into a single bond of love. Marriage is a sacred relationship which should not be engaged without couples receiving counseling explaining marital commitments and requirements. Couples sharing good communication expressions will often maintain cohesion in their marriages and the avenue to better understanding each other.

Chapter 7

Peter and Gloria's Married Life

Peter and Gloria found married life to be complicated and filled with awkward interactions and misunderstandings. Their major problem involved them having difficulties in sharing their thoughts, ideas, and conversations. The exposed troubles in their relationship created unaddressed tensions. This inability to talk to each other and communicate their concerns caused their marital interests to decline. Regardless of the topic, there were conflicts. If Peter said it was a good day, Gloria found fault with his assessment. Whenever Gloria recommended that they do something she thought would be good for their joy and pleasure, Peter could not see the enthusiasm, pleasure, or enjoyment he would get out of it. Their love relationship moved from being warm feelings with joyous emotions, to that of being cold and indifferent toward each other. Their marriage became a contrast between love and resentment. Rather than allowing their relationship to be as two ships passing in the night making love connections, they became like two destructive trains on a collision course.

Peter and Gloria had not considered that their marital relationship would ever engage in conflicts, problems, or unaddressed personal issues. Although they knew some adjustments were needed because of their background differences. However, they convinced themselves that the true love they shared would be enough. At first, they celebrated their diversity and delighted in their differences. However, as time passed, this contrasting thinking became irritants to them in varying ways. Because of these unsettling differences, they soon discovered that many of their conversations ended in arguments. They couldn't say much without the other one critiquing what was said and criticizing the thought process. They couldn't agree on the acceptable tone of respect or how loud the volume should be before it becomes disrespectful. Raised voice. Disrespectful tone. Overbearing presence. If one or the other did either or all these actions, it was determined to be totally wrong. When Gloria would at times speak with a loud voice, Peter labeled her as being hysterical. However, when Peter's voice became loud, Gloria felt intimidated and accused him of trying to dominate or overpower her. If either one spoke in a low or soft tone voice to someone else, whether on the phone or in person, the other one made it seem as though some secret or illicit information sharing was occurring. Yes! They could see that the good relationship they once shared was leaving them. All that they valued at first in their relationship was being devalued by their inability to talk to each other.

Peter and Gloria at first believed their love relationship was a spiritual gift from God. However, the uncertainty of their future together due to the loss of that magnetic attraction they once shared, caused them to consider whether to try keeping their love alive. They no longer shared positive conversations or laughed out loud together. Because the relationship had not lived up to their initial expectations, each one in quietness of thoughts questioned the relationship in their hearts, and wondered "Where did we go wrong?"

Part 2

FINANCES
(Show Me the Money)

Chapter 8

"Financial Planning"

Finance is the second of the four significant elements in marriages which often determine the success or failure of the relationship. Finances or money in marriages is the most significant resources of support by which couples build their lives. Therefore, it is essential for marital couples to develop financial plans which address their lifestyles. Being good money managers would ensure successful financial planning. Money is commonly accepted by most people to be what's required to live, grow, and survive. However, marital couples, when managing and spending money, have differences between being single and married life. Being married requires partnership, understanding, and love. Before marriage, couples were free to spend their monies as desired. As individuals they had complete control and final say as to how, what, when, and where their money was spent. However, at the betrothal altar, they were no longer individuals. In marriages the focus must be about the relationship, about "we," and "ours," and not "me" and "mine." In marriages, it is of necessity that all monies and financial earnings be discussed, agreed to, and planned between couples. This will avoid or negate issues and concerns designed to rob couples of their peaceful relationships. Life would be an ideal world for married couples if they didn't have to worry about money to spend, incomes to live on, or having to save for retirement. Unfortunately, real life requires money to live, pay bills, do other things, and to have joy. However, the joy of married life is more fulfilling than worrying over money or lack thereof. A joyful marriage joined together with love is more satisfying than all money or financial concepts. Marriage is more than a concept. It is a loving responsibility. It is a caring commitment. It is a lifetime opportunity for couples to bond together.

Chapter 9

Financing Marriages

Peter and Gloria came to understand that marriage is a process of loving and learning about one another. This process also involves, at times, painfully wrestling through difficult marital issues and circumstances. Finances are always an important consideration when couples begin their lives together. Spending adjustments must be made. Instead of thinking as one, the consideration must include two. In their efforts to become the loving couple they desired to be, Peter and Gloria came to agreement as to how their monies would be spent. Initially, they thought that they could continue to earn and spend their monies as though they were still single. This worked well for them until the monthly bills started piling up with neither one of them assuming responsibility for managing, accounting for, and paying them. They soon realized that something was wrong with their money management process. Bills notifications for utilities services disconnections became times of finger pointing, name calling, and blame for the conditions they faced. Also, failure to pay their rent on time brought them eviction notices.

As the monthly bills started piling up and not having enough money to pay them, this loving couple began slinging accusations, like flying whirlwinds, at each other. It became evident to them that they had failed to adequately discuss the roles money played in their relationship. This ill-conceived recognition shook up the loving peace they initially shared. The calm and serene atmosphere of their home and relationship was replaced with contentious interactions, worries, and finger-pointing. For a few moments they each felt betrayed by the images, allusions, and concepts of marriage they had been given by people along the way. No one had expressed or talked to them about the significance of financially managing their monies. Being caught financially behind, and having incurred more debts through their individual spendings, they found themselves living from paycheck to paycheck. Living this way, they found little joy in being married. They asked themselves questions such as, how could things have changed so drastically? What could be done to bring happiness back into their home? Is the price for marriage too high a cost to pay?

One of the many problems Peter and Gloria had regarding money management was knowing how much money they had together. Unfortunately, they had adopted the practice of keeping 'secret monies' from each other. That meant, for them, not revealing all their financial resources. Keeping secrets about money in marital relationships is akin to sitting on a stack of dynamite with the stem lit and burning rapidly. It's only a matter of time before there are explosions. Especially when facing difficult financial times. There was no exception to this rule for Peter and Gloria and neither for any other couples who try to hide their valuables from their marriage partners.

Peter and Gloria received bad financial counseling from some of their married friends before they got married. Without having an in-depth understanding of how to financially manage a home, they relied on some of their personal advice about money management to help them. They soon learned that much of what they saw and heard was not what they needed. One piece of advice given to them encouraged marital deception about their finances. That advice suggested that couples should not reveal or share all their money information with their mates. As appealing as this advice was to them, it proved to be unwise information. They learned that this example of financial practice in marital living causes more financial problems. Instead of working together as a married couple, they felt licensed to continue to control their monies like they were singles. This erroneous or deceptive guide to good money management gave them the wrong understanding of how to best manage their monies. Fortunately, they were wise enough to talk with each other about the varied financial information they were getting from their many friends. Their financial troubles resulted from not talking about their money matters. Peter and Gloria learned the importance and value of having a marriage where they could talk openly and honestly about marital issues.

Money management solutions require married couples to talk with each other about managing their monies. In this process, they must be willing to share the worth of their financial resources and agree how they will manage their living. Talking about money management is far different from knowing how to manage money. Effective communication is more than saying, "We talk about things all the time." Shared communication language clears up confusions, misunderstandings, and assumptions. When it comes to financial discussions, couples need to know what they are saying, and each knows what they are talking about. Because if mismanaged, financial concerns can easily and often derail marital relationships. Money talks between couples should focus on marital requirements for maintaining their home and family. This process usually includes paying bills on time, providing amenities and home equities, ensuring effective home securities, and maintaining a wholesome marital atmosphere. However, when couples fail to talk about these requirements or ignore their importance, such negative results as financial dishonesty, secret money accounts, and lack of personal trust occur.

Peter and Gloria were struggling mightily trying to manage their finances. Many family members and friends were putting in their input and giving financial advice. Some advice given was so poorly explained that if they had tried to follow it, their financial situation would have been made worse. As Peter and Gloria struggled to pay their bills, their lives became more miserable each day. They had problems! Problems! Problems! Money problems, living together problems, mismanaged money problems, every-day getting along with others' problems. They were living in misery. They needed relief from the agonies of their financial woes. They blamed their financial problems on insufficient funds, their lack of money. However, as they began discussing their financial situation, they discovered that their true financial problem was not having enough money to support them, rather it was bad money management. When their incomes were calculated together, their combined finances were sufficient to support the needs of their home. Yet month after month, despite possessing sufficient financial resources, they had been struggling to make it work for them. Their major financial flaw was the failure to have a financial plan. This would have made them better money managers. That is why they constantly found themselves in financial binds lacking sufficient funds to meet their needs.

Chapter 10

"My Money, Your Money"

Where is that sure-to-succeed financial formula which will provide married couples adequate resources needed to manage their households? The plain answer is that no such formulas exist! Financially speaking, there is not a one-size-fit-all financial plan which will meet every married couple's needs. That is why couples need to make time to consider their financial needs, spend time developing the monetary plan for their home, and commit themselves to making their plan work. Another way of saying it is that couples need to make their own financial plan, assess the worth of their financial plan, then agree to work that plan together. Before couples start spending their monies, it is important that they understand how much money they have together. Having good money management skills will provide them with financial knowledge of ways to support their home. This financial plan should be based and focused on their marital dreams and goals. Without a clear manageable financial plan couples will often experience extreme money issues and problems. Failing to have a financial plan will result in failure.

Many newlyweds, early in their married life, struggle financially because they fail to plan beyond the pageantry of their wedding ceremony. Beyond the excitement of getting married, couples often overlook or consider how they will live. Instead, their focused attention is usually on sensuous pleasures and the joy of being with each other. Envisioning the full spectrum of marital living is low on their list of considerations. Although many couples do not at the beginning understand their marital responsibilities or comprehend their relationship commitment, it is still important to emphasize that marriage is a joyful experience and a dutiful responsibility. Therefore, anxious couples who are excited about the marriage process without considering living beyond their ceremony can be compared to a young person getting his/her first automobile. Knowing that the possibility of having a car is possible, all this young person thinks about is getting that car. That becomes the focus of his/her interest. He/she is convinced after looking at the price tag that he/she can afford that vehicle. On the surface it appears that the person's calculation for the vehicle is correct. He/she has enough money to make the purchase. However, what the person(s) fails to include in the calculations of buying this vehicle is the cost for operating and maintaining it. These considerations must include insurance costs. The price of gas and oil to keep the vehicle running. Tire repair and occasional new tires. The routine maintenance requirements for that vehicle, and many needed minor adjustments. All these costs exceed the initial price of the vehicle. Servicing the vehicle is essential for keeping the automobile both functional and operational. Just as it is important for drivers to give continuous detailed attention to the care and use of their vehicles, equally so it is important for couples to give such attention to their marriages.

Money in marriages can be a help or it can hinder the growth and development of such relationships. The most effective means of help that money provides couples come through communication and their ability to talk to one another about money matters. Effective communication is essential and will help couples formulate a financial plan supporting their lifestyle. Money is important for building successful relationships. However, at times money can work against the security of married couples. One of the ways that money works against married couples is what can be described as the selfish application of their monies. Perhaps it can be best labeled, 'my money and your money.' There is nothing wrong with this arrangement if the couple has planned for this form of financial management. However, it becomes a super problem when the concept of, 'my money and your money' is used to prevent one partner in the relationship from knowing details of the other partner's complete financial status. This lack of shared financial knowledge often breeds discontentment in relationships. Especially in times when couples are struggling to meet their financial debts. When one partner doesn't know what the other partner is doing with his/her money, how much income he/she earns, and how else the money is spent, it becomes a recipe for mistrust, resentment, and loss of respect.

Chapter 11

"The Money Plan"

All marital plans should begin in discussions with God. For lasting loving relationships to occur, married couples need spiritual guidance in understanding how to live their lives and spend their monies. Peter and Gloria found themselves frustrated over the difficulty of keeping up with their bills and paying them on time. Their major problem was that when they began their marital journey, they failed to make a viable financial plan. Because of this short-sightedness, they soon discovered that although money can't buy you love, not having sufficient funds to meet indebtedness will bring you misery, despair, opposition, and resentment. Peter and Gloria found their relationship, because of money problems, deteriorating into bickering and arguments. One reason they were having money problems was because they were living beyond their financial means. Peter and Gloria, as with most couples entering married life, try to build their marriages at the same level as their parents. They indebt themselves with expensive furnishings for their homes without first counting the cost. Wanting to live at the same levels as their parents without considering that their parents didn't always live at that level. The result often assures that they will have financial problems and struggles. Peter and Gloria's money issues drained their love, joy, and personal appreciation for their marriage.

As their marriage continued to decline, Peter and Gloria found their lives to be more peaceful when they were not with each other. Social distance became a peaceful companion for each of them. Short-lived were those moments because at the end of each day they had to go home. Regrets often accompanied their return home. Things between them had gotten so bad that as Peter left home one night to get something for the next day's work before the stores closed, he thought long and hard about whether to return home. The local stores would close at 10:00 p. m. He was determined to get there before then. Gloria insisted that he just wanted an excuse to get away from her. The many small issues surrounding their relationship became big ones as they failed to express their true feelings, understanding, and expectations. They argued a lot! Over money they argued! Frustrated with the constant negative confrontations and conflicts, Peter got into the vehicle and hurriedly drove away. He could see Gloria standing in the doorway through his rearview mirror and for that moment he was glad to be gone. He knew that he had to get to the store before it closed, but he needed that excuse to get out of the house. He felt like exploding. To him, marriage had become nothing like he thought it would be. At this moment, he wanted out of this marriage! He wanted to be free from Gloria! As he drove down the hill towards the store, he questioned within himself whether he should stop or not. He thought to himself, "Why use my brakes?" His anger toward himself for allowing his home situation to be in such negative condition caused him for the moment to desire to drive past the store. While caught up in his thoughts, he did just that, kept driving.

The time now was 10:30. Peter, having driven past the store, realized that no other stores in his area were open. So, he just kept driving. Instead of allowing anxiety to ruin this alone time, he sought to enjoy his drive. For the first time in a while, he felt free to do whatever he wanted: break the speed limit, drink until drunk, smoke some weed, even pick up a hooker and give her a ride. This freedom of thought he felt gave him the serenity of adventure. He could go anywhere: New Orleans is crowded, Maine never makes the six o'clock news, and

New York never sleeps. However, his adventurous ride was interrupted when thoughts of his money problems, marital problems, and personal confidence problems all brought him back to reality. He couldn't go anywhere! He didn't have any money! He knew that it takes money to do things. It takes money to go places. It takes money to be happy! He selfishly spoke to himself, "I can't do anything. I can't go anywhere. Why should I go back? I am not happy there!" Then his thought took him beyond his own interests. He remembered that it was money concerns which caused heated arguments between him and Gloria. He did not dislike her. It was his frustrations and need for money which caused him to drive past the store. It was not a desire for him to leave Gloria. Finding himself within a few hundred yards from leaving the county, he faced his greatest challenge as a husband. He had to make what he considered the decision of a lifetime. Was he going to stand up and be the man in the relationship? Was he to face his many problems like a man? Would he be willing to work with Gloria to resolve their financial problems? Or would he be a coward and keep driving and live on his own? While he considered his options, Peter remembered that he was no longer a single man. He was a married man with responsibilities. He reminded himself that problems are never solved by avoiding them. He turned his vehicle around and drove home.

Chapter 12

"Money Management"

Developing a money management plan is an essential task which married couples should employ. Although there is not a one-single plan which applies to every marriage, the principle of money management is consistent with order and good financial practices. Peter and Gloria embraced their differences and committed themselves to building their marriage and placing their lives on a foundation of love, trust, and security. They realized that they allowed money or lack of money management to almost destroy their marriage. They had to honestly ask themselves, "Where did we go wrong?"

After much consideration, they agreed that the missing ingredient in their relationship was spiritual. They had forgotten their vows to keep God in their marriage. Vows and the commitment to not allow anyone or anything to come divide them. Unfortunately, poor money management had done just that. A wedge between them caused divorce to become a practical consideration. However, by reassessing the shared love and value in their relationship, they sought God for spiritual strength and knowledge. Peter and Gloria agreed to ask their pastor for counseling. After hearing his words and understanding his guidance they felt better about their lives. The wisdom from this spiritual Sage gave them confidence to believe that they could include God in their marriage with a fresh perspective toward money management.

The Pastor gave them practical counseling on money management. He explained to them the importance of shared agreements on how their monies should be managed and distributed. He emphasized to them that the financial method couples agree to implement in their marriages should be based on them. They will need to determine how well they can and must manage their monies and financial resources. He encouraged them to avoid, as much as possible, excess indebtedness. His counsel encouraged them to share their financial worth with each other, compile their resources, and together determine how to make their monies work for them. The Pastor expressed the urgency for them to establish within their relationship the operational financial system which will meet their needs. He dispelled the notion that it had to be the same money management plan someone else uses. He made it clear to them that their money problems will be affected by the financial plan they decide to use. He told them that the success of their money management would be based on their faithfulness to the plan. The Pastor reinforced the understanding of the fact that a plan is just a plan until it is implemented as an agreed operational activity. The choice for money management planning in marriages depends on how well couples organize their spending. Money management choices for each marriage may fall between these considerations. It could be that a couple may decide to pool their monies into one account, or have separate accounts, or maintain individual accounts with a central pool where bills are paid. The Pastor made it clear to them that it didn't matter which option they chose as their financial plan. The important thing would be the agreement on how they would manage their money. The Pastor told them that they must make this decision for themselves.

In efforts to help Peter and Gloria work out their financial dilemma, the Pastor provided them information about a Christian-based financial workshop which would be available for them to attend in a few days. He emphasized the value of listening to spiritual leaders who loved God and had the knowledge, ability, and capacity for teaching families, couples, and individuals how to biblically put their finances in order. After hearing about this workshop, Peter and Gloria were excited and wanted to know more about this spiritual leader. The Pastor told them of his friendship with him and that he valued his knowledge and teachings. He was confident that they would greatly benefit from what this workshop and spiritual leader had to offer.

The financial workshop instructor and lecturer was identified as Reverend Jerry A. Seay. A highly recommended certified biblical teacher. He was noted for being a spiritual leader with the financial acumen to teach spiritual and biblical principles on money management through God's blessings. His background in financial management included almost thirty years of conducting, managing, and accounting for finances for the Alabama State Missionary Baptist Convention, the Northwest District State Convention, New Antioch Bethlehem District Association, and local church budgets. Through his financial management and teachings, each level of financial responsibilities increased substantially. Especially through his leadership in the Northwest District State Convention, where through his Presidential leadership the church-based ministry achieved greater historical financial growth and monetary collection.

Peter and Gloria were filled with excitement and enthusiasm concerning the financial seminar. This great news gave them reasons to believe that attending this money management session would change their financial conditions. Therefore, after the Pastor prayed with them, they left his office with a sense of peace and gratitude. As the day of the event came, they eagerly looked forward to attending the financial workshop. As Peter and Gloria hurried to get to the seminar an accident between two vehicles delayed them. When they finally arrived at the place of the seminar, the session had already begun, and Reverend Jerry Seay was speaking. Quietly they found their seats and began listening intently and taking notes. Reverend Seay, through his skillfully developed teaching methods and spiritual purposes addressed the topic of how to make money your financial blessing. It was a humbling experience for them to admit their problems in managing their finances. However, Peter and Gloria were glad to hear their interest being addressed.

Reverend Seay's outline of biblical financial management began with establishing this foundational principle, 'God is the source for all finances.' He methodically referenced biblical scriptures which emphasized the spiritual role by which money and all finances have in forming peaceful happy lives: "The earth is the Lord's, and the fulness thereof, the world, and they that dwell therein," (Psalm 24:1, KJV); Philippians 4:19 (KJV) "But my God shall supply all your need according to his riches in glory by Christ Jesus." Reverend Seay's introduction gave participants and especially Peter and Gloria reasons to believe that they would be greatly enriched by what they were hearing. Reverend Seay emphasized that from the biblical perspective, having the attitude for giving is the foundation for receiving God's blessings, "Give, and it shall be given unto you; good measure, pressed down, and shaken together, and running over, shall men give into your bosom," (Luke 6:38a, KJV).

This aspect of understanding financial management was contrastingly different from how Peter and Gloria had come to deal with money matters. The implied thinking that they learned from others as to how to get money, have money, and keep money were based on the colloquial philosophy, "Get all that you can. Can all that you get! Then sit on the can." In other words, keep all your money for yourself. However, at this biblically based financial seminar they were hearing a different philosophy. It was a practical philosophy, a spiritually practical philosophy which emphasized God's plan for financial prosperity based on giving. This philosophy informed them and challenged their understanding of financial matters. However, when Reverend Seay stated that "Giving is a measure of our love and gratitude," they were astonished at the concept of equating giving to that of love and gratitude. Nevertheless, being intrigued, they gain a greater understanding and meaning of financial management. 'Love and giving.' 'Giving and love.' This combination stirred within them feelings of contentment. Perhaps for the first time in their married life they would be able to settle their financial woes by applying spiritual elements in their calculations.

Love and giving are what they heard to be the connecting elements for financial solutions. Reverend Seay noted for those in attendance that many people fail to grasp the importance of giving to receive because they lack the faith to trust God for their provisions. He emphasized that people should place their faith in God for their finances. He told them that the Bible speaks boldly about where your affections must be placed, "Charge them that are rich in this world, that they be not high-minded, nor trust in uncertain riches, but in the living God, who giveth us richly all things to enjoy," (I Timothy 6:17, KJV). "For where your treasure is, there will your heart be also," (Matthew 6:21, KJV).

Reverend Seay's impressive presentation caused the couple to focus their attention on this spiritual model for financial management. The biblical principles of giving back to God as part of financial management and blessings were the understanding they needed. Although the seminar had been a blessing in helping them rethink their money management by applying biblical principles, Peter and Gloria left the session without saying a word to anyone. They didn't want to acknowledge their financial situation or admit that they had not been good money managers. They justified their swift and silent departure with the thinking that a busy and important person like Reverend Seay wouldn't have time for insignificant people like themselves. Even though the seminar was an enrichening experience for them, they felt with so many people there, they were nothing more than faces in the crowd. Reverend Seay's simple and straightforward method of teaching strong biblical principles made all the difference to this couple yearning helplessly for relief from their financial struggles. Although Reverend Seay never heard this couple's voices or their words of appreciation for what they heard, they were thankful for what he had given them. They left the meeting believing in the abundances of God's blessings and were willing to begin the practice of giving as evidence of their faith in God.

At home, Peter and Gloria recounted the spiritual impact they gained at the lecture on the biblical principle for financial management, blessings, and God's plan to meet all their needs. While discussing their options for planning how to better manage their monies using biblical principles, they recalled the biblical story Reverend Seay highlighted at the meeting and how he emphasized the blessings you receive from trusting God. It was the story about a widow woman who was down to her last meal and

God met her needs. To get a better understanding of what took place, they sat down together, opened their Bible to II Kings, chapter 17 in the Old Testament, and read the story aloud. It spoke of a time when the world was experiencing an extreme famine. Zarephath was the city in which this widow woman and her son lived. Because she had no money and little financial support, this made the time more difficult for them to survive. In fact, they were down to their last meal. In response to their needs, the prophet Elijah was sent by God to this widow to meet her needs. The irony of the story is that Elijah didn't have any resources, money or anything else to give her except his faith in God. Elijah, this prophet of God, was a great candidate to speak about trusting God and Him meeting needs. He could speak about God being a provider and how He would supply her needs. He had experienced for himself God's faithfulness to meet his needs. Even through this unusual drought and famine God provided for him. By faith, he trusted God to sustain him. God honored his faith by sending ravens to bring food to him and providing cool water from a brook.

When Elijah became settled by the convenience of food and water being provided to him, God had to dry up the brook to move him from his location. The primary reason for him to leave this space of comfort was because God had a more important mission for him to perform. There was a woman, in another location he needed to meet, know, and act on by faith. It was her faith which prompted God to respond to her situation, hear her prayers, and meet her needs. After God dried up the brook, Elijah was told to go to Zarephath to continue receiving his food supply. God told him that He had "Commanded a widow woman there to sustain thee," (I Kings 17:9b, KJV). When Elijah saw the woman gathering wood to cook, he asked her for water. She explained to him that she was preparing to cook the last meal for herself and her son. This widow's response would have most likely been baffling to an ordinary person believing they were following God's command. Perhaps these thoughts would have persisted. "Didn't God say that this woman would be able to sustain me? How could she provide for me if she is down to her last cup of meal?" This was not Elijah's thinking. This was Elijah, the prophet of the true and living God. He had too much experience with God to doubt His purpose. He didn't know how God would keep His promise, but he trusted God's process and methods to provide. He told the widow woman to cook the bread, as she had planned to do, but give him some first.

Peter and Gloria paused their reading to discuss and digest what they read. Perhaps these were some of the thoughts or expressions they shared or were thinking. "Well now, what would you say about this? An old man wanting to take bread out of a child's mouth!" As cruel, selfish, and insensitive as this prophet's demand may have sounded to this widow, in a time of famine, and poverty, this request was spiritually deeper than normal thinking could perceive. Elijah's request to be fed first was less about hunger for bread, as much as it was about faith and trusting God. This prophet was not just some man looking for a handout, he was God's man. He represented God who sent him there with the understanding that the widow would sustain him. How could he be out of order if he was following the Master's directive? There are lessons to be learned here! The teacher was not Elijah. The teacher was not a widow. The teacher, as always, was God!

Lesson number one: Always put God first. Lesson number two: Always keep God first. Lesson number three: Always make God first. For when you put God first, all other things come together in the right order. The widow obeyed. According to her faith, God kept His promise of providing for her needs by keeping her meal barrel from becoming empty and her oil from running out. Spiritual success is about faith and giving. Giving is the momentum to spiritual success which faith provides. "Give, and it shall be given unto you; good measure, pressed down, and shaken together, and running over shall men give into your bosom," (Luke 6:38a, KJV).

After reading this biblical account Peter and Gloria understood that God will provide when people obey His word, follow his directives, and trust Him to meet their needs. They realized the significance in them giving to God first. They learned that through good communication, working together, and having an effective financial plan, their future will become a joyful journey to live. They agreed that their financial plan would focus on giving to God first. He is the source for all their benefits.

Chapter 13

"Money Talks"

Stan and Maria, unlike Peter and Gloria, did not seek help in trying to resolve their money management problems. Instead, they buried themselves in debt as they tried to create a home life like that of which they had known growing up. They spent more money than they could afford on things they wanted rather than patiently buying the essential things they needed. They also felt a little embarrassed talking about their money matters with other people. To them, talks about money and family matters should be limited to the family. Yet they found it difficult by themselves to make their monies work for them. Rather than seeking counseling or discussing ways to make their incomes work for them, they got deeper in debts through the access of credit cards and quick loans outlets. These short-term answers to their money problems proved not to be the solutions they needed.

It wasn't long before the pains of debt caused agony in their relationship. Soon they began to resent each other and blamed the other for their financial problems. The joys of marriage had instead become nothing more than living with pain, hurt, accusations, and regrets. Because of poor money management, monthly bills were consistently late. At times one utility or another was turned off due to non-payments. Food in the house was often scarce. At times being limited to bread, beans, and rice. There was never any extra money to buy new clothing for either of them. Periodically, when they thought no one was paying them any attention, they would shop at the Goodwill clothing outlet. Little money and lack of resources meant they couldn't afford to go out or have a regular social life. Frustrations from their financial woes and limitations in being able to do many things robbed them of the joy and happiness they thought life would be for them. Reluctantly, they allowed their circumstances to bring them to the conclusion that they would be happier apart or separated than to remain in these conditions. Perhaps better said, they decided to get divorced. However, before any movements were made toward getting divorced, they decided to talk things over. During their sharing time they found joy in the dream they had for their marriage and relationship. They remembered that it was love which brought them together and despite the agony of their financial problems they still had love. They still believed in their marriage, and they still wanted to build their lives together.

This pause in their decision to get divorced to discuss and reassess their marital relationship was what they needed to prevent their separation. They had allowed themselves to fall into the concept of comparison living. Comparison living had been the major culprit of their financial problems. Ashamed of their common backgrounds, they tried to live at higher socioeconomic levels than their parents. They were determined not to allow the stigma of coming from poor neighborhoods to embrace or define them. However, their money problems were bringing them down, and the desire to quit was hanging over their marriage. Yet, before they called it quits or divorce became a serious topic, they decided to stay together and have a serious money talk. Money concerns had clouded the major thing (love) and caused them to focus extensively on the minor thing (money). Stan and Maria realized that getting into debt was easy, getting out was difficult. Therefore, they agreed to seek help. They decided to no longer allow pride to keep them from overcoming their poor financial management skills. They were directed to the financial seminars conducted by Reverend Seay. Soon they understood the process of giving, having faith, and loving God would meet their needs, order their lives, and keep them together.

Part 3

SEX AND INTIMACY
"What's Love Got to Do with It?"

Chapter 14

"Loving with Honesty"

Sex and Intimacy is the third of the combined elements which often determine marriages' success or failure. It is perhaps the most notable indicator of martial strengths or weaknesses, alongside couples' romantic embraces of each other. Sex being the physical engagement of the relationship, often dominates the immediate emotional connections between couples. It provides them with unsustainable explosive sexual pleasure during the early weeks and months of the consummated relationship. However, when sex and sexual stimulation are motivated primarily by the physical engagements, its pleasure, enjoyment, and satisfaction often lessen in its appeal as time passes. The physical connection between couples, although pleasurable, will eventually reveal some parts missing for lovemaking fulfillments. Sexual fulfillment requires more than being physically engaged. Fulfilled sexual relationship embodies tenderness, expectancy, romantic urgings, and expressed wanting which are immersed in intimacy. Intimacy is perceived to be a partnership between physical and spiritual sexual connections. Couples who are consumed with only immediate physical sexual pleasures soon discover that aspect alone is not fulfilling.

Without intimacy being part of the lovemaking process, sexual pleasure often loses its lasting effect. When couples make physical sexual connection the epitome of their pleasure fulfillment, they soon realize their need for intimacy. Without intimacy being part of their lovemaking, couples will often find themselves drifting apart in search of meaningful sex. When marriages reach this level couples usually do one of two things. One, they will either explore ways to make their sexual life more exciting or two, become engaged in the game of 'pretending'. They will pretend to enjoy being in the engagement. They will pretend that their romance is satisfying and fulfilling. They will even pretend to reach orgasmic fulfillment. Such actions and attitudes will not promote martial harmony. Rather it will often cause them to become socially distant from each other. When couples fail to honestly share their sexual frustrations with each other, they will in many ways become disconnected.

Married couples which lack intimacy in their lovemaking will often experience sexual and emotional failures in their relationships. Intimacy is the love-glue placed in hearts to build, bond, and fill all the spaces where emptiness resides. Without intimacy, lovemaking remains a physical activity only. Something will always be missing. If intimacy's role is unrecognized as a needed involvement in keeping marriages stimulated, the physical aspects of sex will soon become limiting in expressions and disappointing in performances. Intimacy is the reflection of a deeper fulfillment and firmer embrace of that which will provide greater pleasure to physical engagements. As in most marriages, couples' expectations of sexual fulfillment will be in their physical attractions to each other. They soon discover that intimacy is the most sensitive and fulfilling aspects of lovemaking.

Misnomers about sex's impact on relationships often include the belief that it will keep the love-fire burning, maintain couples' loving interests, and remain a desired activity in the marriage. That may be true for a while. However, sex without intimacy in married life can be described more like thinking you are fully dressed when you put on your shirt, tie, and coat, while leaving your pants hanging in the closet. Soon it would be discovered that something was missing. Intimacy in married life is a bonding element which merges differences of perspectives into appreciative understanding. Intimacy involves opportunities for stimulating romances which leads to sexual pleasure and fulfillment.

Another aspect of sexual fulfillment relies on couples sharing honest conversations between them concerning both things pleasant and unpleasant during sexual activities. The need for love and desire for sexual fulfillment and satisfaction for married couples do not automatically occur. Nor does it happen without deliberate efforts from couples. Sexual fulfillment happens when couples come together because they value their marital relationship. Together they must understand that if their marriage is to survive, they must honestly share their sexual needs and expectations. Their sexually fulfilled relationship must include intimacy. When couples fail to express their need for sexual intimacy and settle for just having sex, they soon discover that sexual interest in their marriages will begin to decline. Therefore, before eyes start wandering and minds start roaming, couples need to have good, clear, and intimate sexual conversations. During such sharing times questions about sexual intimacy should highlight the discussions. These questions should include the following: Do we as partners recognize that a sexual problem could exist in our marriage? Have we honestly discussed sexual intercourse importance in our marriage? Have we assumed that our sexual participation is pleasurable? Or that we know how to adequately perform? Do we give sexual satisfaction a second thought after we climax?

Sexually unfulfilled marriages can often be traced back to couples' failures to communicate their need for passion and intimacy in their bedrooms. Couples that are not comfortable talking with each other about intimate matters will often not know how to express their sexual needs or concerns. Therefore, couples' unspoken sexual needs will continually leave them sharing an unsatisfying bedroom. Also, they will make room for influential excuses to explain the absence of their sexual fulfillment. This is one reason why in a sexually social culture where sex products are used for artificial stimulation, sexual fulfillment remain a satisfying pursuit. These misleading indicators as means for attaining sexual fulfillment become more destructive than enhancement of marital relationships. These cultural outlets such as secular music, provocative movies and videos, and explicit reading materials support sexual activities designed to entice couples of all ages to become active sexual participants. There is an assumption that newlywed couples are mentally and physically prepared to engage in meaningful and lasting sexual involvement. However, without couples talking with each other about sexual pleasures, many will become disappointed in their sexual activities. Therefore, if couples are to achieve sexual ecstasy, honesty must connect their lovemaking embraces.

Honesty in marital relationships opens doors for true expressions, needed intimacy, and opportunities to address concerned issues. Whenever couples dance around issues or the truth concerning their sexual needs, they run the risk of weakening their marriages. When married couples' sexual relationships fail to stimulate their needs along with the refusal to talk about their sexual needs, temptations will come to entice one or both to seek fulfillment outside the marriage. The importance of honesty includes being willing to speak plainly about what is pleasurable, comfortable, and preferred methods of intercourse. Honesty is truthfully caring enough for your partner to reveal or admit to him/her what sexual activities, positions, interactions, or engagements may be painful, discomforting, or lack the intimate connections to stimulate. Relationships which fail to make honesty the foundation by which they address or discuss personal issues, topics, and concerns risk losing in each other both confidence and trust. Without shared honesty in sexual matters, trust becomes suspicions which will erode love in the relationship.

Having courage and personal confidence to talk with your partner about sexual matters, or preferred sexual positions, or sexual methods are needed actions to attain sexual fulfillment. Without such courage to address these sensitive areas, expressions in the relationship will result in dissatisfaction. Lacking courage to speak the truth for fear of becoming subjected to shame, ridicule, or disappointments from your partner will leave you in a troubled relationship. Fulfillment rests in personal confidence. When couples share their confidence to provide stimulating sexual performances, their lovemaking will often explode into intimacy. This kind of personal confidence has the power and ability to bring together sexual needs and spiritual fulfillment into eroticism. Confidence, therefore, becomes the required strength couples need to live together! Confidence of this kind will provide genuinely shared love with tender embraces and higher levels of pleasure! Through their emboldened shared love marital couples' homes and lives will stand in difficult times. Love which lasts and sexual needs met are platformed on honesty. Sexual honesty dispels false assumptions and will provide daily opportunities for intimacy and fulfillment.

Chapter 15

"Night Of Martial Bliss, Or Not"

Peter and Gloria learned to appreciate the concept of loving with confidence. After extended periods of feeling sexually incomplete, they agreed that knowing about sex and participating in stimulating sexual activities were quite different from knowing about how to have sex. Sexual discouragement for them began on their honeymoon night. Contrary to their anticipated night of out-of-this-world lovemaking which would explode like Fourth of July fireworks, this special night ended in disappointment. It became more like a rained-out picnic. At first, they were unsure as to how to discuss the disappointing situation. They feared that one or the other may wrongly interpret any inquiry or explanation given. Still, something needed to be said, made known, or spoken aloud! Lacking the courage to address their concerns, the couple remained silent. However, as time passed, it became obvious that something was either wrong or totally missing from their relationship. Unwilling to discuss their intimate problems, Peter and Gloria's relationship remained painfully absent of needed intimacy. Their inability to talk about marital problems was causing their marriage to fail.

Chapter 16

"Lady With A Smile"

Years ago, there was a prominent lady in her community who was well-loved and respected by all who knew her. She smiled often and did not mind helping people whenever she could. Yet behind her smile was a woman desperately in need of love and appreciation. Although she was married, her relationship with her husband left her sexually unfulfilled. Her greatest obstacles were finding the answer to her problem of needing sexual fulfillment. A major obstacle she faced in this struggle was how to overcome her lifelong teachings about a woman's sexual role and attitude concerning it. During her youthful years, sexual participations and expectations for women focused on pleasing men more than seeking pleasures for themselves. Sex in marriages for women at that time was perceived to be a woman's duty to perform. Therefore, many women were left sexually unfulfilled. Many women didn't feel like they had the cultural freedom or voice to express their need for sexual intimacy and personal fulfillment.

Early in adult life being married did little to change the sexual restrictions she had experienced and observed women of her era enduring. She was married, had children, was well liked, and respectfully thought of by people in her community. However, as she approached middle age, she still hungered for this qualifying sexual fulfillment. During her youthful days women were made to feel that their sexual role, duty, and responsibility was only to provide pleasure for men in their lives. Often these women were left sexually unfulfilled. They were not culturally permitted to question their sexual activities, their roles in sex, and their lack of sexual intimacy. Sex for women focused on satisfying the men. Therefore, men and women rarely spoke openly about sex or sexual matters. The subject was an assumed understanding of what was supposed to happen, take place, or endure. Sex was assumed to be what couples did without explanations. Sexual performances and positions were already established and determined with missionary being the primary one.

Enough said about that barbaric period for women and the conditions they had to endure for sexual pleasures and fulfillments. Women from such generations were led to believe that sex was more of a duty for them, and not so much as acts of love or pleasure. Women's role and position in such relationships were to sexually please their men. It didn't matter much if women were left sexually unfulfilled.

One day this woman, in much frustration, visited her pastor and shared with him her honest longing need for love and sexual fulfilment. The Pastor asked her "What was wrong with her sex life? What was it that she needed, wanted, looking for, or thought was missing in her marriage?" Sadly, she admitted that in her more than 30 years of marriage, she had never had sexual pleasure with her husband in their bedroom. When the Pastor inquired deeper into the proposed problems, he learned that this couple's sexual position was the main reason that sex was a concern. She admitted that her sexual life had not only lacked intimacy, but it was also a very discomforting and physically painful engagement for her. The hesitation for her in confronting this problem was that she didn't know how to talk with her husband about it. She didn't know how to be honest about this very personal and sensitive area of marital life. She didn't want to bruise his ego or make him feel like something was wrong with him or her. Certainly, she didn't want to anger him and lose him. Therefore, she remained quiet through the years and endured the pains.

The Pastor was a little perplexed because he had known this couple all their married life. He performed their ceremony. Every Sunday, he would see them and conclude from their appearances that they were a happy, loving, and fulfilled couple. This insight into their marriage was baffling, yet it was his duty to provide this dear lady, his church member, with some words of relief. "Daughter," he said to her, "the answer rests with you. I could tell you to try this or that, but you alone know what you need and how to get it. So, my advice to you is to be honest with yourself. Be strong in your convictions. Have courage to meet your concerns head-on. Above all, don't do something that will cause you any embarrassment, if you know what I mean." She knew what he meant. He didn't want her to stray off in some vile direction seeking fulfillment. She left the Pastor's office feeling as unfulfilled as she did before she went in to see him. She even felt a little ashamed as though she had violated the sacred secrets of their home. She wondered whether she had made a mistake talking to the pastor. Will he look at them differently now? Will he think less of them? Her? Nevertheless, she found solace in her efforts to do the right thing. Unfortunately for the betterment of their relationship, her husband never knew about this intimate concern, and she remained sexually unfulfilled. She confessed that she often thought of seeking pleasure outside marriage, but never found the courage to do so.

Chapter 17

"Loving with Confidence"

"Loving with confidence" was a phrase that caught Gloria's ear on her way to work one morning as she listened to her favorite radio station's praise and worship program. It was the voice of a seasoned Christian woman who was known in the community as being a great Bible teacher. This seasoned saint was Sister Pearline. She was not a woman preacher, nor did she try to imitate or pretend to be one. She was a teacher of God's word. She embraced that spiritual calling with all the authority heaven scripturally provided her. Her focused teachings and interests were on helping women and children to know God and how to live godly lives. Her God-anointed calling to this ministry duty came one day while reading her Bible. She had a spiritual hunger and desire to do something for the Lord. She earnestly wanted to know how she may become both a vital and valuable servant of the Lord. She did not want to be, nor perceived to be one who engaged the ministry as a preacher. She had observed far too many people limiting God's calling to serve as their opportunity to be identified as preachers. That was not for her. Yet, she knew God was calling her to a special ministry service. The revelation of what she was being called into became known to her from the Bible. It was in the Book of Titus, written by the Apostle Paul to one of his spiritual protégés. Paul sent this young preacher, Titus, to a city named Crete with this instruction, "For this cause left I thee in Crete, that thou shouldest set-in order, the things that are wanting," (Titus 1:5a, KJV). It was what Sister Pearline read in chapter two that set her ministry in motion. It was instructions to older or mature Christian women, "That they may teach the young women to be sober, to love their husbands, to love their children, to be discreet, chaste, keepers at home, good, obedient to their own husbands, that the word of God be not blasphemed," (Titus 2:4-5, KJV). From that moment on she understood this purpose to be God's calling of her into the teaching ministry. Her spiritually ordained work would be to women and children. Therefore, each morning, on her radio program, she provided encouragement to women who were in troubled marriages, unsettled relationships, and to those seeking spiritual understanding of God's purposes for them.

REV. DR. LORENZA JAMES

This morning as Gloria was listening to Sister Pearline's broadcast on her way to work, she found herself with tears flowing from her eyes. She was hurting. She needed more than she was giving and receiving in her marriage. Peter was the man she loved! Peter was the man who brought purpose to her life! He has been the man for her from the moments and time they met and fell in love at the Quiet Stream. Those moments shared at the Quiet Stream were special and sacred. The Quiet Stream was their personal place of discovery. It was where they came to know one another. It was the place where love became a personal commitment. It was as sacred of a place to them as was the spiritual pool of Bethesda, a Bible story found in the Gospel of John, fifth chapter. This sacred pool was a place where sick and hurt people gathered daily hoping for a miracle. People with various diseases, sicknesses, personal issues, and various other health conditions were brought there with the motivation of trying to be the first one into the water. The legend concerning this pool was that periodically an Angel from God would come down and stir the water in the pool. The first person into the water would receive immediate healing of whatever ailment he/she had been affected. Few were healed. Many were not. Yet they continued to come to the pool with the hope and small expectation of being that one who would receive the healing. In this Bible story there was a lame man of 38 years who received a personal visit from Jesus who asked him the most important question anyone seeking healing need to be asked! "Do you want to get well?"

The Quiet Stream, as was the Bethesda pool, perceived by many as a meditative place of hope and healing expectation. People came there seeking peace, safety, and restored personal confidence. This Quiet Stream place was sacred. It brought healing to hurting relationships, restored hope to those wading in lost hope, and renewed focus to those seeking greater purposes for their lives. It was at the Quiet Stream that Peter and Gloria found each other. They had previously experienced rejection by their lovers. They went to the Quiet Stream where they sought and found each other relief from the pain, stain, and agony of being rejected in love. However, unlike the man at the biblical pool who received that personal visit from Jesus with that liberating question, "Do you want to get well?" Peter and Gloria were attracted to each other by the hurt they felt in their hearts. Their sadness, evident by their facial expressions, was like magnets drawing them together. It was as if they were being asked that same question as the lame man in the Bible, "Do you want to get well?" The man in the Bible offered excuses as to why he couldn't get healed. Jesus refused to entertain his reasoning. Rather, He simply told the lame man to get up and walk.

Peter and Gloria couldn't explain why they each felt attracted to the other. They simply took it to be a special message of healing from the Quiet Stream. The calm atmosphere, like a gentle breeze blowing from the waves, brought serenity to their lives. They felt and appreciated the magnetism which drew them to each other at the Quiet Stream. Peter and Gloria found a secure connection whenever they embraced each other. They shared a loving affection, and a grateful appreciation for the opportunity they were given to love again. It was at the Quiet Stream that their love relationship began. This love motivated them to get married. However, they discovered that feelings of love alone were not enough to satisfy their unfulfilled sexual needs. Like many couples they didn't know how to talk about their sexual problem. They didn't want to hurt, doubt, or have misunderstanding to rob their relationship of love. They wanted and needed confidence with courage to express their sexual failures and needs. What good is love spoken between couples if they are unable to feel the fulfillment? What good is love when it becomes a routine bedroom activity without the energy of passion? What's love got to do with it?

Chapter 18

"Putting Things in Order"

The day moved slowly for Gloria as she worked on her tasks. Sister Pearline, from the morning radio program, was in her thinking all day. She needed to hear more about putting things in order. She loved her husband and didn't want their marriage to end or fall apart. She could sense the dangers their relationship was facing because of their poor sex life. As she contemplated making an appointment to talk with Sister Pearline, she wasn't sure as to the best way of doing it. How would Peter feel about her going or would he be willing for both of us to talk with her? If she went alone, would he feel that she violated the sanctity of their home or relationship? However, after much debate with herself Gloria, knowing that something must be done, decided to go alone. If it helped her, it would be helping them. If it did nothing to improve her understanding of how she must address or deal with their sexual concerns, she would be no worse off. She made the appointment for Wednesday night, 6:00 p. m., Bible study night. She knew that Peter would be at church. They went to church services and Bible studies religiously. She would make some excuse not to go this time.

Sister Pearline could tell by Gloria's cloaked approach with her that this troubled young woman had sexual problems, issues, and concerns. Their brief introduction, and cordial small-talk conversation soon became more serious as Sister Pearline delved into the true reason Gloria was there. "You are having bedroom problems, aren't you?" Sister Pearline asked. Gloria sheepishly responded, "Yes!" Sister Pearline gently encouraged her to talk about it. Not knowing exactly how to openly speak about her personal and private issues, she burst into tears. "I love my husband, but I don't know how to fulfill his sexual needs." It took courage for Gloria to admit out loud that she had sexual problems in her marriage. Sister Pearline, having a tender concern and empathetic ear listened intently to Gloria to ensure that she was there to help. She used this moment to provide Gloria with consoling counseling which would give her a new perspective and a spark of hope toward solving her bedroom problems. Gloria's honesty about her situation caused her to graciously receive Sister Pearline's inspirational instructions, guidance, and understanding as to how to make lovemaking with her husband a more pleasant engagement. This comforting process and therapeutic information dried up her tears and brought a smile to her face. This spiritual counseling gave her peace and relief from her concerns.

Sister Pearline, in this holistic session, gave Gloria a hand-held mirror and asked her to describe what she saw. At first Gloria thought this was a ridiculous suggestion or exercise because she knew what she looked like. Nevertheless, she was encouraged to look more intently at the person she was facing in the mirror and described what she saw in loving intimate terms. Gloria, at first had difficulty in trying to find the right words to describe herself. Sister Pearline, coming to her rescue, recognized that her innate problem was that she didn't see herself as being a beautiful, desirous, or intimate person. Sister Pearline explained to Gloria that lovemaking was more endearing than a prescribed process or designated positions. Intimate lovemaking involves couples' perception of themselves, their shared relationship concerns, and a willingness to accept one another for him/herself. She emphasized to Gloria that one reason couples have bedroom problems is because they often accept what other people say about sexual interactions. She explained that couples must determine for themselves as to what activities motivate their sexual engagements. Sister Pearline reminded Gloria that sexual pleasures are neither based on the size of partners' sex organs or their participating positions when it comes to lovemaking. Although much attention is given to sexual appeal, intimacy often ignores sizes (big or small, wide or thin) for the benefit of satisfaction. Sister Pearline emphasized to Gloria that it is what's done to attract sexual interests which should be given the most attention. It is the attraction for intimacy which will hold couples in lasting loving embraces. That is why sex must be understood as being shared expressions of couples' love for each other. With this understanding, times shared in sexual bliss will always create explosive pleasures.

Sister Pearline insightful counseling of sexual interactions gave Gloria the renewed energy she needed to go home and work to resolve her marital and bedroom problems. As Gloria made herself ready to leave, she thanked Sister Pearline for the session which had taught her the value of having positive self-esteem. However, before she reached the door, Sister Pearline called her back for one more bit of information. She shared with Gloria her faith and relationship she had with God through His Son Jesus. She lovingly told Gloria of her love for doing the Lord's work. She believed that it was her mission and ministry to tell women, especially young women like her, what God wants them to do with their lives and their bodies. Therefore, she told Gloria to value her marriage, to never use sex as a weapon of control, or punishment. She pointed out that the Bible makes clear the duties of the husband and wife when it comes to sex. Sister Pearline referenced for Gloria the scripture which spelled out husbands and wives' duties in marriage. "The husband should not deprive his wife of sexual intimacy, which is her right as a married woman, nor should the wife deprive her husband. The wife gives authority over her body to her husband, and the husband also gives authority over his body to his wife. So do not deprive each other of sexual relations," (I Corinthians 7:3-5, NLT). Gloria understood the message, although she didn't think it really applied to her problem. Nevertheless, she thanked Sister Pearline for such an enriching time. She left for home feeling motivated to make intimacy the heart of her marriage and sexual pursuit.

Chapter 19

"Husbands Love Your Wives"

It was the same Wednesday night on which Gloria went to see Sister Pearline and Peter went to church alone. Normally he and Gloria would be there together. Tonight, he welcomed being alone. Gloria had given reasons for her not to be at church. Instead of being troubled over the split Peter utilized this time as needed personal moments for himself. He found solace in being at church this night. He needed help. Spiritual help. All that he wanted in his marriage seemed to be there. All the pieces fit together should be enough. He had a good woman, a nice home, they had prosperous jobs, and for the most part a good home atmosphere. All the pieces. Yet, for some unknowable reasons, the pieces were not fitting together. He knew that he and his wife were always talking to each other, but not always communicating. Their lack of shared word meanings created misinterpretations and misunderstanding many times about what was being said or discussed. Something was missing. The kisses they shared had come to be without only tenderness. Their warm and loving touching of each other had become nothing more than extended cold love taps. Without sexual intimacy, the relationship's sincere emotions had become empty feelings with hollow expressions.

Peter prayed at the altar for change, understanding, and peace. As he thought about how much love he had for Gloria tears flowed from his eyes. The Pastor came and knelt beside him. In a soft supportive voice said, "Let's talk." They went into the Pastor's office. There, in deep spiritual conversation Peter shared his consternation over his home-life and marital woes. He shared with the Pastor frustrations he and Gloria were experiencing. Despite all the good they had in their marriage, they seemed to be falling away from each other. The Pastor, without wasting words with any type of relationship analysis, told Peter that God expected him to be the man in his house, husband to his wife, and the lover needed in their marriage. Peter was stunned at how direct the Pastor's words to him were. He was expecting a different approach to addressing his concerns. The Pastor had closely observed Peter and Gloria's marriage since the day they got married. He said to Peter, "I know where you are in your marriage, and

I know why you are growing apart." Peter sat there perplexed asking himself, "How could he know anything?"
The Pastor went on to speak about the aspects of married life without making it a dialogue. He told Peter that
a strong marriage begins with the biblical understanding of marriage. Marriage is God's ordained connection
between a man and a woman. Marriage was instituted by
God when He created Adam and Eve, the first family and
placed them in the Garden of Eden with this understanding. "Therefore, shall a man leave his father and mother,
and shall cleave unto his wife: and they shall be one flesh,"
(Genesis 2:24, KJV).

Peter knew about the story of Adam and Eve in the garden of Eden, but he didn't understand what that had to do
with him preserving his marriage. The Pastor recognized
that his point was being missed. Peter was half-heartedly
listening to the Pastor because his mind was focused on
problems he and Gloria were having. He was concerned
with this troubling question, "Where did we go wrong?"
The Pastor continued to throw-out biblical and spiritual
references about marital relationships. He shared with
Peter the counsel of the Apostle Paul in Ephesians chapter
five, verses 25-31. He cautioned Peter to listen intently
because in marriages God holds the husband's responsibility sacred. He spoke to Peter about the marital responsibilities which couples should know. "Husband, love your

wives, even as Christ loved the church, and gave himself for it," (Ephesians 5:25, KJV). Even after hearing another scripture from the Bible Peter seemed perplexed as to the meaning and correlation between what the Pastor was talking about and his concerns. Totally exhausted by what seemed to him like prolonged senseless information about marital relationships, Peter interrupted him asking, "Pastor, what are you talking about? What does all this have to do with me? I love my wife. I care for her. I try to make her happy. What am I doing wrong?"

The Pastor leaned back in his chair, looked Peter directly in his eyes, and informed him that to love his wife as Christ loved the church required of him at least three things: Love her unconditionally. Love her sacrificially. Love her continuously. He asked Peter, "Are you willing to love her in these manners?" Before he allowed Peter to answer, he further explained what these areas of love meant. "To love your wife unconditionally, as Christ does the church, means that you are not looking at your wife to find fault with her; even when some of the things she does may not be done the way you would do them. Unlike in early biblical days when God through Moses' teachings, permitted men to divorce their wives for anything they didn't like (Matthew 5:31-32). Husbands today should not look for reasons to not love their wives. Divorce was never part of God's plan for marriage. The next thing is unconditional love, which simply means for you to never stop loving her. Sacrificial love means that you, the husband, should put the needs of the wife before meeting his own needs. God's purpose for having husbands to love in these manners so that he may provide his wife the joy, happiness, peace, and feelings of security she needs to feel loved. Continuous love is absolutely what it says, love continues through difficult times, challenging times, and most importantly, quitting times. The husband is what the Bible calls the 'Strongman' of the house, 'When a strong man armed keepeth his palace, his goods are in peace,' (Luke 11:21, KJV). It is an awesome responsibility that every man must consider before he decides to be a husband."

Finally, after listening intently to what the Pastor was trying to get him to grasp and understand, Peter quietly nodded his head to acknowledge what he was hearing made sense to him. He understood that his primary responsibility as a husband is to love his wife. Loving his wife! That thought continued in his mind as the Pastor prayed God's blessings for him, his home, and his marriage. Peter left the church and headed for home. Peter loved his wife, but he didn't know how to love her to satisfaction. He knew what needed to be done, only he didn't know how to do it. All the way home his focus was on being better in all categories his marriage required of him.

Chapter 20

"Sex-Appealing"

Sex and intimacy are needed partners in achieving sexual fulfillment in marital relationships. Communication is not limited to spoken words only. It also involves understanding the ways people think and their actions. It involves understanding how sexual stimulations differ between men and women. This needed grasp of sensuous information includes acknowledging that men and women generally approach sexual intercourse from different mindsets, different motivations, but with the shared expectation for sexual fulfillment. For instance, men are more stimulated by the visual, what they see. On the other hand, women are more process oriented, and instinct guided in their sexual drive. Men are more easily aroused by suggestive sexual images. Women's sexual motivation requires time, attention, and feelings of being desired and wanted. Men often approach sex as something that they do. Women perceive sex as something that they give. Therefore, without intimate communication in their sexual relationships, couples will often find themselves frustrated, unfulfilled, and reaching the stage where one or the other want to cheat, they both cheat, they desire to quit the relationship, or all the above. Among these reasons is the understanding that sex alone does not have the enduring power to sustain marriages. Sexual fulfillment demands time, sincerity, and intimacy. It is the kind of intimacy which is felt deep within. Intimacy applied to the lovemaking process will give participating partners the desired chills, thrills, and stirs up heated emotions which express their passionate love.

Sex is a subject guided by differing opinions of what it is, how to perform it, and what must be done to share in its pleasures. For years, perhaps maybe always, sex has been considered, by some moral elements of society, to be a restrictive public topic for discussion. For those conversations, sex was both sacred and taboo at the same time. Sacred because God designed sex to be expressed and shared in the sanctity of marriages. To provide married men and women sexual pleasures. Taboo, because in social settings sex is presented in some public discussions to be nasty and dirty topics. It is perceived by some as private moral subjects which should be done inside adults' homes.

This mindset was one of several ways and methods used by adults, and specifically parents to discourage their children from prematurely engaging in sexual activities. It was their efforts to encourage their young people to pre-serve and reserve themselves until marriage. These parents were desperately concerned with preventing their children from premarital pregnancies. They wanted them to main-tain their options and freedom to choose a future without the restraints of teenage indiscreetness. It was also con-sidered taboo for adults to entertain each other sexually before marriage or become sexually involved with some-one other than their spouse after marriage. Because sex was considered a quiet topic in public discourses, many people often spoke of sex, in social settings, with smirks on their faces, or grins on their lips, or quiet whispers in someone ears, deeming it too private for open discus-sions. Contrastingly, sex in past societies was considered a restrictive subject or unacceptable topic for public discus-sions. However, in recent times sex has become culturally implanted into everyday living and has become common parts of social dialogues. In this sex-focused world, many citizens are active participants in sex-laced language to the inclusions that many conversations and general talks are accepted as societal norms.

In the world of commercial marketing, sexual topics and images have become tools and instruments by which products are exploited and sold. Such items include clothes, food, cars and trucks, and generally anything that is for sale. Sexy models are often used to sell and market cars and other automobiles. Food products as well are sexualized for better sells. Social culture has absorbed sex as an appealing standard for living. Citizens can't get away from its influences. Therefore, when men and women form their personal relationships, their desired sexual appeal has already been commercially influenced. However, after a period of engaged sexual activities, couples come to the realization that sex-alone is not strong enough to sustain their relationships. Initially, sex is like a magnet for couples. They are sexually engaged at every turn. They can't get enough of each other. After a few weeks, or a few months, maybe six or seven at the most, couples often discover that sex-alone is not enough. Occasionally, this lost appeal often causes couples to seek stimulation in other interests. For some, the needed interest for attention leads them into extramarital affairs. Others distract their need for sexual fulfillment by engaging in activities, events, and services which give them a sense of satisfaction and personal worth.

Peter and Gloria recognized that the major flaw in their sexual relationship hinged on their inability to communicate with each other. They, like many other couples, assumed that sexual interactions were as natural as the breath they breathed or the winds in the air. However,

Peter and Gloria's personal talks with Sister Pearline and the church Pastor provided them with greater awareness of how men and women differ in expressing and attaining sexual fulfillment. Couples are often hesitant to entertain questions about sexual fulfillment or engage in sexual discussions for fear that their partner may misunderstand the discussion and become emotionally hurt or feel rejected. Nevertheless, couples seeking wholesome martial relationships need to understand how to sexually please and pleasure his/her partner. This conversation needs to include without fear of failure, loss, or disappointment as to what has sexual pleasure and what is not pleasing. Couples must not assume or try performing any unusual sexual acts or activities without his/her partner's agreement or approval. This approval should be based on shared love, comfort, and desire. Before various sexual positions and methods are tried or introduced into marriages, couples should agree to such endeavors and are willing participants. Couples' sexual experiences prior to the shared one with his/her marital partner often determine their confidence and freedom in expressing sexual changes. It is best for the relationship that couples talk about their sexual experiences without naming names or numbers. However, couples must be aware that discussing previous sexual experiences could create greater problems of insecurity, feelings of competition, or being compared with prior lovers.

Sexual problems in marriages are often rooted in the history and backgrounds of marital couples. When couples are uncomfortable with sharing past sexual experiences for fear of being unaccepted by their marital partners, they don't talk about previous sexual activities. Couples must understand that intimate details of past relationships are not always required for engaging in various sexual acts with spouse or current partner. Information about past sexual endeavors should be carefully engaged and not treated as though it is a normal conversational topic. There are many dangers in bringing up or discussing relationships prior to being married. Among them are comparisons and jealousy. When comparison is the issue men, more often than women, they feel challenged in the bedroom. He more often will wonder if he measures up with past lovers. He will be challenged to doubt whether he possesses the ability and tools to fulfill his woman's sexual needs. Comparison between the past and present becomes the albatross around necks of lovers feeling insecure in their marital relationship. Questions revolving around their marital insecurities become their daily mental exercise. He asks, "Am I the one she wants?" She wonders, "Does he desire me as much as he did her?" He thinks, "When she's with me is she thinking of him?" She considers, "Does he think I am prettier than his other women?" Over and over the comparison carousel between their inward thinking turns. Because they fail to find comforting grounds to discuss their sexual problems, the proverbial cycle continues, problems develop, misery becomes the companion of these distraught lovers.

Children and young people are introduced to sex in somewhat crude ways. Some by watching how adults behave. Some who observe older siblings engage with their friends. Some are given fairy tales understanding of what sex is all about. The birds and the bees are one such example of adults attempting to explain the engagement. However, the discussion of sex and introduction of sexual principals differ from one family to the next one. This difference poses a dilemma which often is based on how people get and form their understanding about sex. That is, what it is and how to do it to get the greatest amount of pleasure. For example, one family may speak openly about sexual matters while another family makes discussion of sex a quietly spoken topic. One family has sex to be an open discussion while another family has sex being a forbidden topic of discussion. For this reason, couples' discussions of sexual activities must be understood from their respective families' teachings, warnings, and restrictions. Families' moral teachings and social mores about sex differ from house to house. That is why when couples are experiencing sexual problems, they must be willing to discuss the topic of their sexual involvements. They must understand their differences and willingly agree that their sexual discussion is about them and no one else. Couples who leave sexual questions lingering between feelings, methods, or lack of stimulation often find themselves with more sensuous bedroom troubles. Understanding how to relate more intimately with their partners requires couples to learn from and about each other. "Do you enjoy sex?" "Are you willing to learn different methods and positions?" "Do you prefer doing sex in certain ways?" These are but a few sexual questions which may aid couples in realizing how to pleasure their partners. Sexual activities must be weighed against their sexual instructions, sexual under-standing, and sexual awareness. This topic of concern often goes back to couples' growing up days. The times in which boys and girls were made aware of their sexual differences. Without clear explanations about their bodies' physical differences, they were merely told as developing boys to keep their private parts private. Do not show the opposite sex that private part. This unclarified restriction only heightened curiosity for many young people trying to discover themselves. Not always knowing why they could not openly share their private parts with the opposite sex, these boys and girls pursued this "forbidden zone" of phys-ical interaction and discovered unrealized pleasures.

The precautionary warning, "Don't do it," which was intended by caring parents to restrict or prevent early sexual contacts between boys and girls, instead ignited more curiosity about sex. In quiet pursuit this curiosity caused many young people to enter these forbidden or restricted zones often when left home alone, or visiting neighbors' homes, or overnight stays at family and friends' houses, or on an occasional date. Sometimes young people deliberately defied parents' restrictive command to "not to do it" and became sexually active. Ironically, human beings are peculiar in this manner. Whenever people are told not to do something, a defiant and resistant attitude rises within them stimulated by their curiosity of the forbidden zones.

Peter and Gloria's sexual history was along such guidelines. They had engaged in sexual activities but had never really grasped the fulfillment of what they were doing. Perhaps their lack of understanding of sexual fulfillment may have provided the rationale or contributed to their previous love relationships failures. Perhaps it was the main reason that their lovers rejected them. Since then, they have a better understanding of the significant role sex has in keeping relationships vibrant. Having gained this knowledge of sex importance, they had confidence in their marriage to build their lives together. Their past failures and assumptions about sexual activities taught them the importance of being willing to talk about sex with your partner for better understanding and greater sexual fulfillment. Although Peter and Gloria gained new insight,

REV. DR. LORENZA JAMES

awareness, and understanding toward solving their sexual problems, they still had to work on repairing their marriage.

They agreed that if their marriage was to be renewed, it needed a fresh start. Therefore, over a cozy romantic dinner they met at their favorite restaurant which was located near the Quiet Stream. On this evening, they shared loving moments of intimacy which enclosed them in a sweet conversational embrace. Their early evening dinner ended up being a joyful late supper. The evening was filled with delightful memories of their shared love. Peter asked Gloria to remember his love for her and how much he cared. He spoke eloquently about the beauty he found in her appearance and how the warmth of her personality made him feel special. He told her that from the first moment they engaged at the Quiet Stream, he considered her to be his "Dream Girl." He expressed how blessed he felt having her in his life. He believed that God made her especially for him.

Gloria, not to be outdone, also used recognized flatteries to acknowledge her love for Peter. Her words spoke tenderly of the moment she remembered when they shared their first embrace at the Quiet Stream. She said that it was as if she was falling into darkness with no hope until his embrace brought her back to life, secured her feelings, and restored hope in her heart. Her expressed love for Peter echoed the words in Roberta Flack's song, "The First Time Ever I Saw Your Face." Gloria referenced selected words from the song which spoke of the loving impact Peter made in her life. Then to Peter's surprise, Gloria started singing the song, "The first time ever I saw your face, I thought the sun rose in your eyes, and the moon and the stars were the gifts you gave to the dark and endless skies, my love, to the dark and endless skies. And the first time ever I kissed your mouth, I felt the earth move in my hand like the trembling heart of a captive bird. And the first time ever I lay with you, I felt your heart so close to mine, and I knew our joy would fill the earth, and last 'til the end of time."

Knowing the depth of love Peter had for her, Gloria affirmed her love for him. She joyfully emphasized to Peter that not one moment of the day passes without him being in her thoughts. That he was the difference between love and emptiness in her life. She concluded with this unanswered question, "Where did we go wrong?" Before she permitted Peter to give an answer, Gloria thought about the wise words and spiritual time she spent with Sister Pearline. She reflected on the revealing truth the mirror Sister Pearline gave which helped her understand how she viewed herself. With a nervous sounding voice, Gloria asked Peter this direct question, "Do you find me sexually appealing?" Peter was stunned by this direct question.

He was unprepared to respond to this sensitive inquiry. He wasn't sure what to say. He contemplated as to what would be the right or appropriate answer! How would his answer alter their very warm, tender, and positive shared conversation? Nevertheless, he trusted the intimacy of this shared moment to say the right words. He prayed that it would not alter the positive setting they were enjoying. His answer was "Yes!" The tone of his voice affirmed that his answer was true, real, and could be trusted. He assured her that there could never be a finer looking or more appealing woman for him than She.

When it comes to fixing relationship problems, couples can take one of two pathways: they can play the blame game and remain hostile toward each other, or they can with loving courage, speak honestly about the issues they face. Peter and Gloria decided to take the honest pathway to discuss their major relationship concerns. Although they feared the possible dangers of further damaging the marriage by speaking honestly about some things, they thought it necessary to speak the truth. They had come to believe that doing anything less would not only damage their flailing relationship but could also end their marriage. They understood that this was the time for honesty. If truth couldn't save their marriage, being untruthful would not hold them together. Slowly their conversation led them to reveal what stimulated their romance and what gave them pleasure.

They agreed that their sexual attractions for each other had waned because very little was done in the bedroom to stimulate their interests. Having taken for granted their intimate times together, they stopped making special efforts to capture the love, attention, and sensuous moments required for stimulation. Instead of wearing intriguing, alluring, and enticing lingerie or sexy boxers, their appearances had become unattractive with no appeal. They once cared about their intimate appearances and were concerned with how they looked. Their personal attention had been to their attractive physical appearance. Early in their marriage they were consciously aware of the need to look good. It was a qualifying motivation. It kept them interested in each other. It drew them closer together. However, when marital and housekeeping problems piled up on them, their interest in sex and sexual fulfillment became less appealing. They stopped dressing up for each other. They forget that physical appearances were necessary stimulants for sexual appeal.

When Gloria asked Peter's opinion as to whether she was sexually appealing to him, his hesitant answer concerned her. He was careful that his answer would not hurt her feelings. At the same time, he didn't want her to think that he was just saying what she wanted to hear. Peter was aware of Gloria's insecurity with herself because of her increased weight, but that neither affected or diminished his love or desire for her. It really didn't! He truly loved her for who she was and what she meant to him. However, they like other married couples, allowed their love relationship to fall into a state of complacency. A developed attitude of apathy. At the beginning of their marriage Peter, after coming home from work, would clean himself up to ensure that the odors of his workday did not stink up the house or smell up the time he spent with Gloria. Unfortunately for them, their relationship got to the point where he stopped caring about his looks or bad smells. He stopped making any adjustments. He constantly used the excuse of being too tired to do anything but go to bed. He learned afterwards, through their many conversations, there were things they had taken for granted or ignored. As a result, their relationship was no longer fresh, pleasing, or desirable. One big turn off for Gloria by Peter was his not cleaning himself up before any attempts at intimacy or having sex. His bad body odors became a difficult scent for her to accept. His loving embraces were cancelled out because of his awful body odors. The stale aroma of his musty day turned off any sexual interest she might have had or wanted from him.

Gloria, although bothered by Peter's odorous persona, had not given him any reasons to know or believe that his body odor was offensive to her or a problem at all. Her silence about this issue kept him clueless that his body odor contributed to their bedroom concerns. Peter had wrongly assumed that her love interest had changed and placed her affections somewhere else or on someone else. After hearing what Gloria said about his appearance and body odor Peter understood her resistance to him. Their conversation made him consciously aware that sexual appeal in the bedroom must involve deliberate efforts to look sensually good and smell invitingly good. Body cleanliness and appealing appearances seem to have been the heart of this couple's sexual problems, which on the surface should have been small and easily resolved issues. Yet, it is quite clear that when truth, honesty, and a willingness to talk about troubling matters, little things, irritations, and annoyances can become big trouble in marital relationships. Whenever couples fail to communicate with each other about things large or small which irritate them, misunderstandings often occur. That is why couples need to speak honestly to each other about issues which may annoy them before these small annoyances begin eroding the joy of love and intimacy they desire in their relationships.

Peter, after hearing what Gloria said about him, became convicted of his habits. He apologized to Gloria for his insensitivity and at that moment renewed his vows to love her. He committed himself to being more physically and spiritually aware of what and how to meet her needs. He wanted Gloria to know that she was his one true love for the rest of their lives. After holding Gloria's hands in his hands, he then laid them on his chest next to his heart. He then assured her of his love, acknowledged that he understood where they had gone wrong! He promised to never allow their marriage to go that way again.

However, before Gloria would permit the curtains to fall on past mistakes, empty moments, and regretful encounters, she wanted Peter to tell her why he no longer had attractions for her. Was it connected to how she dressed, increased weight size, or her low self-esteem? All Gloria needed was to feel loved, wanted, and desired. She told Peter that without his loving arms to embrace and comfort her, she didn't always feel convinced that he still loved her. This uncertain feeling often contributed to her developed jealous attitude. Silently she felt emotionally abandoned and accused him of being unfaithful. "Tell me what you think has gone wrong with us? Or relationship?" She earnestly sought his response. She wanted to know what took his love away from her.

Peter's affirming words of love brought tears to Gloria's eyes and joy to her heart. His tender words assured her that his love for her had not changed and would never change. He admitted that there were problems that needed to be addressed. However, her physical size or weight were not a concern for him. Peter's lighthearted expression brought a smile to Gloria's lips when he said that her gained weight was not a turn-off, but a turn-on. He lovingly told her that her size gave him more of her to love. The problem which bothered him was her bedroom attire. It was how she dressed for bed. Gloria was baffled by his statement! She asked him to explain why the way she dressed for bed was a problem. Peter shared his frustrations by telling her that bedtime to him was an intimate time. It is a time for reaching out, coming together and being stimulated for sexual pleasures time. It is an intimate time for couples to engage in passionate lovemaking. However, Peter told Gloria that instead of their bedtime being intimate sharing time, it had become the opposite, a turn-off time because what she wore to bed didn't set the mood for sex. Her pajamas and cotton socks made the mood for sex less appealing. Instead of putting on dainty lingerie which would stir his interest and desire, she often would wear some kind of unappealing clothing to bed.

Peter told Gloria that the message he got from her bed clothing was basically "Don't bother me." Or "I'm not in the mood!" He said that whenever he reached out to touch or embrace her, he often felt rejected. It made him feel that either she didn't want him or didn't believe that he wanted to be with her. He felt that his efforts to be intimate with her was either not genuine or not appreciated. Therefore, Peter assumed by her cold response to his efforts to make love that Gloria had the impression that he was just going through the motions, pretending. That his actions were done merely to keep peace in the marriage. Gloria was horrified to hear how Peter characterized her actions, her attitude toward lovemaking, and her lack of sexual intimacy. With tears in her eyes, Gloria apologized for the erroneous messages Peter had received or perceived about her desire to have him or be with him. She reaffirmed her love for him with the promise that she would do her best, from this time forward, to always be appealing to him. She expressed passionately her love and respect so that he would understand that he was her man. The only man she wanted, desired, or loved. Gloria's affirmed commitment to Peter was joyfully received.

After Peter and Gloria expressed thoughts about their marital problems, they embraced and agreed to fix their marriage. This renewing process became a time of connecting, closeness, and healing the hurt they've felt in their marriage. With renewed interest and attraction towards each other, their evening concluded with them involved in tender lovemaking and sexual bliss. It was the kind of Fourth-of July experience they both had longed to share. During their discussions Peter and Gloria learned many things about how to maintain the fervent heat of love and intimacy in their marriage. Among them was their commitment to always be honest with each other and to make good communication a priority in all their discussions. They realized that being honest about marital issues and not being afraid to talk about them were the key to their marital restoration. They realized that when they apply intimacy to their sexual times, it will cause their marriage to be strong, lasting, and reflective of the kind of love that will keep them together.

Part 4

FAMILY AND FRIENDS
"It's A Family Affair?"

Chapter 21

"Support Groups"

Successful marriages are components of loving couples, healthy living environments, and strong unintrusive family and friends support systems. This is the fourth member of the combined elements which married couples need to effectively apply to make their marriages truly the life they build together. As with all levels of marital relationships, much of what is effectively done depends on how well, how much, how alike couples communicate and relate to each other.

Couples are joined together in marriages to build their future together. However, they do not come into the relationship detached from their past histories or previous relationships they were involved in. They also bring along with them their marriage's family connections, friends associations, and other acquaintances. These family members, friends, and acquaintances have emotional attachments and dedicated interest in each member of the marital partnership. These loving overseers become protective coverings and avenues for couples to seek their counsel, advice, and/or outlets to vent. Because couples are loved by them, these groups want to ensure that the husband and wife are well cared for and properly treated. However, as important as these needed support groups may be in assisting married couples, they can at times be hindrances to couples' family development. Without intending to be negative influences in any way, they may at times contribute to couples' marital problems. Therefore, to avoid such results marital couples must talk with each other and agree to the involvement of family and friends in their married lives. Through this agreement couples will avoid many well-meanings, but at times unneeded negative marital inputs. Instead, they will be able to incorporate positive interactions from these needed support groups. When couples fail to talk about and agree to the extents these valued relationships will be involved in their marriages, they will often find themselves in conflict with each other over such matters.

Chapter 22

"Family & Friends"

F amily generally consists of people who know you, love you, trust you, and support you. Family is often accepted as being the foundation of strength by which dreams are launched and hopes are secured. Family relationships are extensive, loved, and appreciated. Family connects brothers and sisters who are endeared to each other. Siblings are family members who usually grow up together. As with all family folks growing up together, there were times when brothers and sisters irritated each other, got mad at one another, and played mean tricks on one or the other. When the deed was done against you, not only did it grate your spirit, but it also made you wonder at the time how you could stand to live with them. However, after having grown up together, and having shared the same family experiences, these family connections become valued bonds treasured in your heart. Family folks are people which you can criticize, say negative things face to face about them, and they will still receive your love. However, let no person outside of the family circles utter any disparaging remarks about any family member without them feeling the wrath and response of the family.

Peter and Gloria valued their family interactions and welcomed them participating in their marriage. The lessons they learned about family caused them to value their involvement in the relationship. It occurred during the early times of their marriage. They had the misconception of what must be done to keep family peaceably involved in their lives. Therefore, every time someone called for or planned family activities or events, they felt obligated to be there. Often, such family events would conflict with their previously made plans. Soon their attitudes toward family events became resentful for having to attend and participate in them. Although a grievance, they didn't say anything to anyone about it, not even among themselves. The reason being is that when it was Gloria's family which interrupted their planned event, Peter would reluctantly go along with silent resentment and malice in his mind because of the event. Although he didn't say anything about it, he even resented Gloria for them having to attend the event. However, whenever Peter's side of the family invited them to participate in family outings which interrupted the couple's scheduled activity, Gloria would find reasons not to go. Realizing that her absence from attending Peter's family events would cause strife between she and Peter, she half-heartedly involved herself in his family's doings. Usually, after the events had begun, she would use the opportunity, when presented, to justify reasons for her early departure. She neither liked the events nor wanted to be part of them. She would not speak of her dislikes to Peter for fear that he would be offended.

Neither Peter nor Gloria disliked their partner's family. The problem for them was that often their families' planned events and activities came between what they had planned for themselves. Without consideration, they were expected to be at all family occurrences regardless of whether they had plans of their own or not. This problem of dealing with families' events had become a complex concern. They had conditioned themselves to remain silent rather than voice to the event planners their own interests, concerns, and desires. Neither Peter nor Gloria wanted to give either family the idea or indication that they didn't like being with them or wanted to participate in their family events. Their problem wrested with them being unable or unwilling to say aloud what they felt in their hearts. They had a communication problem. The solution to their dilemma was simple, they needed to talk to each other. As they refused to step out on that limb for fear that it would cause them greater pain with each other, they continued to ignore this divisive issue. However, as time would reveal, things didn't get better by not address-ing the problem. Finally, Gloria said it out loud, "We have to talk!" Peter agreed.

As Peter and Gloria talked about their families' involve-ment in their marriage, they were pleasantly surprised that both had the same thoughts about the situation. They recalled the things that the Pastor said to them during their pre-marital counseling. He told them to keep their families in their hearts but keep them arms' length away from being involved in their marriage. His reasoning was that marriage often is a perceived relationship projected to others in two visible forms: One being like a camera's snapshot and the other being more like a developing movie. The snapshot version is what people outside of the marriage see and hold onto as their view of the relation-ship. This is one reason why couples should hesitate to include family and friends into their marital discussions, issues, troubles, squabbles, arguments, or disagreements. The problem with snapshot moments is that they could become lasting negative images and resentful attitudes about one spouse or the other. Snapshots are not complete pictures or lasting stories. Nevertheless, resentment, bit-terness, or sometimes hatred of that person could be the results based on the photo-image of the relationship by family and friends.

Married couples have conflicts. They get upset with each other. They walk out. They call each other hurtful names. They cry and threaten to end relationships. However, because this is an ongoing movie relationship between them, and not a snapshot moment, soon after the spat that caused the disruption has been given time for reconsideration, they recover from their anger, forgive one another, and return to loving embraces. That's the difference between the two projections. Therefore, married couples need to love their families and friends. Family and friends need to continue to love them back without interfering with their marital disagreements.

Peter and Gloria agreed that sharing time with their families was important for them. They needed that family-touching interaction. However, they knew the significance of reserving personal time for themselves. They valued the families shared times where fun, relaxation, and precious memories were established. These family activities caused them to appreciate each of their families. Therefore, to keep peace with families they agreed to share time with their families, but reserve times for themselves. Peter and Gloria's wise agreement showed love and appreciation for their families' involvement in their lives. However, they also valued their decision to maintain time for each other. For them to make their own family history, they needed time to be alone. Personal time. Intimate time. Personal times which in years to come would reflect valued memories. Family, love, and working together are elements couples have relied on to build their marriages.

Friends and friendships are valued relations married couples need to have, and to share. Friends are needed for strong social connections and emotional support. However, when such relationships are not quantitively measured their presence and involvement in couples' time may negatively impact their interactions. For example, when people who are friends with married couples and they do not recognize couples' need for time alone, infringe the friendship by being inconsiderate. Such awareness will often strain such friendships or end them altogether. To avoid losing friends or having conflicts in marriages because of friends' invading interactions with them couples should discuss and agree on friends' social association. Far too often married couples incur conflicts in their relationships because they assume that their mates have no objections to them spending time with their friends when they could have been with them. Marital conflicts rooted in misunderstandings are often found to be based on assumptions. Therefore, to avoid misunderstandings and unhealthy conflicts among friends, couples must be honest about friends' roles and involvement in their relationships.

Friends' involvement in couples' marriages must be an agreement. This agreement can include predetermined times, activities, or events couples permit themselves to share with friends. Involvement, communication, shared understanding, and agreement are elements required for healthy friendship relationships. For example, if Gloria, without having communicated with Peter her desired schedule for the day, went shopping from early morning to late in the evening with her female friends, this could cause conflicts in the marriage. Assuming something not being a problem often becomes a problem. Without prior understanding and agreement, Peter would have grounds to be upset with Gloria. Truth of the matter, without understanding in marital relationships, such inconsideration would most likely cause problems in the marriage.

Assumptions can become destroyers of marriages. For example, if friends of the wife, without consulting the husband, take her out and keep her away from home until late in the evening, assuming that it will be without conflicts. These friends' lack of consideration disrespects the home and marriage of this couple. Friends are valuable, but when time spent with them is prioritized to be more important than being with your spouse or home, friendship becomes too high of a price to pay.

Equally so! Best buds of the husband who spend long hours at his house are inconsiderate of his time with his wife. There are times when pals can relive their past experiences but should never be at the expense of the marriage. When friends assume that their long-time visiting is not a concern, this assumption often sows discord and yields troubles for the relationship. On the surface such actions by friends would seem innocent of any conflicts. After all they are just friends. However, when friends drop by unannounced or come over without being invited or stay too long when they come over and nothing is said or done to stop such actions, this becomes a family problem.

When husbands permit their best buds to stay long hours at their homes, leaving them to assume they can stay as long as they desire, this becomes a faulty assumption. Marital couples must always keep in mind that home is their sacred living place which belongs to each of them. Therefore, all activities and invited guests into their homes need to come with shared approval. Without this consideration from each partner their home will become a place of marital contentions. Couples must reserve the rights in their homes to maintain respect for themselves, one another, and to reject anyone's failure to respect their space or place. This even includes disrespectful friends. The home must always be valued by couples with the right to reserve their personal and private spaces.

Friends' involvement in married couples' lives must be agreed to by each partner. When certain friends disrupt married couples' lives, home, and/or relationship, association with those friends must be dismissed. However, when married couples' friends are respectful and remain positive contributors to the relationship, they are friends which couples can agree to share their company.

Chapter 23

"Divorce Is Not a Shining Star"

Couples experiencing intimacy problems in their marriages often find their sexual involvements becoming routine physical interactions. Lacking the courage to address this problem with intimacy, they start finding faults, making excuses, and drifting apart. Fear of being hurt or misunderstood are among the main reasons couples fail to acknowledge this intimate problem. The result is that the problem remains unresolved. Delaying discussions of marital intimacy brings no solutions. The emptiness of lovemaking because of deprived intimacy will often lead to delayed pains, hurts, and rejections. Soon the relationship will become degraded to the level where either thoughts or actual suggestions will be about separation or divorce. However, before divorce discussions occur, couples should reassess how sacred marriage is for them, and how much they value it. These reevaluation discussions become opportunities to consider the consequences of divorce.

Contrary to what some may believe, divorce is never a gentle process of departure and separation. Divorce becomes more often like the hunger of a raging tiger towards its prey. It brutally devours relationships. Tearing the life out of marriages and leaving the remains of a once loving connection torn into many pieces. Divorce is a torturous pain and agony process. It brings discontentment and discouragement. When couples are faced with divorce, they must consider how their lives after this process will be affected. Discontentment will influence their decision toward a better life. Discouraged couples will not find in whatever divorce settlement the peace, comfort, and safety they seek for themselves. Divorce is a world of opposition. Divorce is a present danger when marital mishaps occur, and an uninvited guest which brings negative conclusions. Divorce! No matter how smooth a separation may be at face value, no matter how amicable the picture of kindness the process may present, no matter what impressions others may have about couples' separations, divorce remains a painful process. It always leaves scars (seen and unseen). Rejections scars. Incomplete feelings scars. Thoughts of failures and defeats scars. Other emotional scars are evidence of divorce destructive tornado-like damage done to marriages. Divorce is the after-effects of brokenness in marital relationships. It is a record of love, loss and respect. It the moral decay of sacred vows made to be faithful until death.

With understanding that God ordained marriages to be lasting covenant relationships between men and women, divorce must not be considered a celebratory decision. Neither its acts, nor its activities, or events. Many couples involved in the divorce process incur various negative conclusions about their life worth, their ability to love, and their relationship with God. It is here in these considered moments of marital separation that prayers are needed to cover divorce pains and disappointments. Thoughts of divorce and separations for some couples are painful, discouraging and humiliating feelings of shame. The actions of separation rob them of their peace of mind and cause them to conclude that nothing seems to matter or have values worth pursuing. Couples reaching this point in their relationships need to know that regardless to what else may be on their minds, if they believe in God, it's prayer time! Prayer is often found to be the comforting answer to marital mishaps. Without utilizing the strength and power of prayer, divorce's emotional impacts on couples often leave them indefinitely damaged negatively.

Divorce is a moral decision reflecting the decline of marital trust. At best it can be described as a failed partnership. Aside from being in an abusive marriage, divorce has never been sanctioned to be a good solution. However, in abusive situations, divorce may serve as the best outcome. Divorce is a disappointing final act for couples' interrupted dreams of shared lifelong relationships. Therefore, when marriages break down and divorce is couples' constant topic, the process of them building their lives together soon ends. Divorce forfeits couples' shared love, intimate feelings, emotions, and sexual desires. It should not be used as a threat, a force, or a power when marriages are struggling through dividing issues. Divorce is a bitter pill of discontent which should not be used to overcome perceived irreconcilable differences.

Couples whose marriages seem determined to end in divorce should make every effort to understand what went wrong with their relationships. During this evaluation time, they should seek to know where and when disconnections between them occurred. While searching for answers to their marital dilemma, they need to explore possibilities for them to mend and restore their relationships. Divorce is an option for all troubled marriages. However, couples should not use negative or profane words against each other to justify them getting divorced. Dissensions between them should not be given power to allow divorce to have the final say. Reconciliation possibilities should be included in the discussions. A revitalized relationship may be gained through responses which involve kindness, respect, forgiveness, and second chances. The reasoning is simple. Before changes can occur in any situation truth must prevail. These honest expressions of pent-up emotions, unwanted behavioral acts, and all decisions that have influenced or impacted marriages need to be spoken from the heart. Circumstances which caused the hurt, pain, and misunderstanding must be positively settled. Remember, divorce was never intended to be the final word in any marriage. Neither by God who established it, the pastor who married them, loving family members and friends who showered them with love and blessings, or even couples themselves who thought their marriages would last a lifetime.

Stan and Maria came to the realization that married life is a valued world of possibilities needing to be discovered and encircled by love. It is a treasure worth seeking and pursuing after. The love attraction on which their relationship began proved to be strong enough to keep them together through their times of struggles, misunderstandings, and other obstacles they faced. They came to realize that marriage is more than a ceremony. It is a joining process between couples desiring to share their lives, love, hope, and possibilities with each other. When faced with contentious situations which included rumors of infidelity, money issues, or other family issues, instead of seeking approval or acceptance from others outside of the marriage, they embraced each other, believed each other, and stayed together. They wouldn't allow the thoughts of divorce to be final. They believed that they had enough love for each other to sustain them through whatever difficulties they may face. Still, they had marital problems and divisive issues to address.

Maria came from a strong religious background. She prayed often. Her prayers during those early days of marital troubles provided her strength to endure the ridicules and verbal abuses Stan directed toward her. He was extremely negative towards her which caused much tension and conflicts in their marriage. It appeared that after each skirmish or argument they had, words from them would echo sounds which suggested that they should either break-up or end the marriage. These marital conflicts would always leave Maria with hurt feelings and low self-esteem. Although pains from these negative interactions caused her to feel weak, she was determined not to quit. Instead, she relied on her religious background, training and discipline to control her impulses to respond negatively to Stan. Rather than trading insults with Stan, she offered him joy and peace she had from her spiritual relationship with God. Although Stan was not too receptive to this religious stuff Maria wanted him to know that it was through God's love, strength, and power that she was able to endure his verbal abuse and still love him. Stan, not being a religious man, resisted her efforts to push God on him. Instead, Stan mocked Maria's belief in God by calling her faith nothing more than, 'spiritual babbling'.

Stan's background and upbringing was quite different from that of Maria. The neighborhood he came from was considered by normal societal standards to have been rough, tough, unsafe to live, and with the assertions that nothing good comes from it. People with tough or bad reputations were considered the class of the 'Camp' as people in his neighborhood called their location, and they wore that stigma as if it was a badge of honor. Stan's rough and sometimes insensitive way of talking to people reflected the influence his environment had on him. He learned how to survive in it. Therefore, his background was a tattered pattern of troubles, struggles, and evasions. For him, life was rough, raw, and a great challenge to survive. The violent atmosphere, constant negative actions, and the protective attitudes of people in his neighborhood demanded that he be tough. He had faith. Not some spiritual faith based on any religion or God. He didn't have time to put much belief in a God he could not see. His life survival skills were dictated by this street code, 'fend for yourself and don't trust anybody else.' That is why when it came to Maria sharing her faith and love for God (babbling he called it) Stan was not ready to hear or receive it. To Stan, Maria's conversations about God was nothing more than religious noises. Spending time praying to God for needs, help, or anything to him was wasted time. He felt that there was no profit is placing yourself or having faith in a God you can't see, touch, or prove his existence. Stan was reluctant to embrace Maria's God and her faith. She constantly invited him to join her in going to church or spending time with her in prayer. Stan couldn't grasp the concept of how God being centered in his life would provide him safety and security. Still the impact of Maria's devotion to her faith raised questions about his thinking. Such questions included: would faith in God stop others from shooting at him or bullets from hitting him? What about being safe in your own house? How will believing God keep thieves from breaking into your houses or beating you up? Therefore, Stan summed up his willingness to believe in God in one word, No! As far as he was concerned, he was willing to leave this God talk and God belief to church-going folks. It was not for him.

Unfortunately, Stan had based his desire to believe in God on his observation of church folks who spent time praying to God, but had no love for people who didn't go to church. To him, this hypocritical parade was nothing more than religious games played in the name of God. He saw these people as being nothing more than love talking, loud singing, and long praying folks who were no better than people they criticized. From his observation many of these people always going to church were nothing more than pretenders. These negative images of church peoples' faith in God were more than Stan could embrace. He saw no spiritual values in worshipping this invisible God. Stan's commitment was to himself for survival and not some invisible God.

Despite their struggles and clashes over religious beliefs and practices Maria had a loving influence with Stan which caused him, in his own way, to give thoughts to having a personal relationship with God. He could see that Maria was committed to her faith. Even though he made fun of her devotion to this invisible God. Without being overbearing and demanding that Stan embrace her faith in God, something happened. Her quiet influence worked. A spiritual change came into Stan's life. Exactly what did it, only Stan knows. The moment or hour the change occurred, only Stan knows. Nevertheless, it became evident to Maria and others by his changed attitude that Stan had become a believer in God. He had come to possess a personal understanding of the God he had labeled a concept, an 'invisible being' that was a waste of time to believe existed. Many wondered who could have caused this staunched rejector of God to now profess faith in Him. The speculations were many. Perhaps he had a dramatic attention-getting encounter with God which caused him to examine his heart. Such as the one which was experienced by the Apostle Paul on the road to Damascus. Paul's spiritually blinded eyes were opened to the truth about God (Acts chapter 9, KJV). Perhaps his encounter with God was a quiet surrender to the revelation and acceptance of Jesus being the expected messiah. His curiosity perhaps the same as was Nathaniel when told by Philip that they had found the Messiah. When Nathaniel questioned the statement, Philip merely told him, "Come and see," (John 1:45-46, KJV). Or maybe he was just willing to accept God's invitation by faith to spiritually know Him. Such was the calling of Jesus earlier disciples, Peter, Andrew, James, and John, fishermen who were asked to become his disciples and follow Him. Immediately they dropped their nets, left their boats and followed Him into discipleship (Matthew chapter 4, KJV).

Or perhaps it was simply Stan's weariness from fighting without and within over God's existence. He needed spiritual relief. He lacked peace of mind. Perhaps this is what caused him to seek God for himself. His life had become a process of dealing with difficulties. Daily he wrestled with anxieties, depressions, and low self-esteem. He soon realized that his mental state was taking him dangerously to levels where he could lose all he loved and valued. Most importantly were thoughts of losing his beloved Maria and their marriage. This fear of loss was based on the many struggles he and Maria had over resolving issues in their marriage. This consternation caused him heart-felt sorrows and troubled mind over thoughts of Maria leaving or divorcing him. He believed that losing her would leave his life and home empty of love. He had wrestled with the concepts of right and wrong, truth and pretense. He was all confused trying to live in two worlds of standards. He loved Maria, but nothing was going right. He needed to love her and to be loved by her, his wrestling with issues caused him inward turmoil. Their marriage for him had become more like torture than pleasure. Stan had no peace. He agonized over his pain. Divorce seemed to be the only way out of this confusing maze he was caught up in. He needed peace of mind. Stan's troubled mind caused him to think of losing Maria, his treasured love. It appeared to him that what he thought would be a partnership journey had turned into a one-way street toward loneliness.

Stan was ready to quit and give up on the relationship. Then, to his surprise, he felt tender loving arms embracing him. The feel of this warm securing touch calmed his fears, doubts, and anxieties. Maria whispered in his ears, "Love is stronger." Although he was familiar with the sound of Maria's voice, on this day, it sounded different. The softness and kindness of her spoken words pierced through his apprehensive thoughts, changing his mind and his life. He felt assured for the first time in his life that love and this marriage he so deeply valued could be trusted. He turned and embraced Maria. His broad smile showed that he agreed with her assurances, 'Love is Stronger.'

Love is Stronger than efforts to deceive, destroy, deter, or under-mind what God has ordained. Therefore, couples contemplating the painful process of divorce should take time (personal time, spiritual time, some alone time, serious time, and honest self-evaluation time) to examine and analyze their marital differences. Afterwards, they should consider the effects decisions to end marriages will indefinitely alter their lives. Times used in martial discussions of issues by couples are important. They should never be viewed as useless exercises or wasted time. Making time to discuss and understand what happened to the love which brought them together is significant and not wasted time. This love must be considered stronger than anything that comes to separate them. It must be stronger than any obstacles which come to divide. Stronger than any efforts designed to destroy meaningful moments of intimacy. Stronger than all other outside entities which seek to interfere with the love, growth and development of marital relationships.

Married couples who are considering getting divorced but are still trying to work through their marital issues need to utilize each moment as a shared opportunity to discuss their differences. It is through such discussions that marriages are strengthened, and marital problems are confronted. This process often becomes the difference between staying together or moving farther apart. Troubled marriages are often in urgent need for couples to give their personal attention to their marital issues. Therefore, couples must make every effort to save or preserve their marriages. This includes recognizing that now is the time to do all that can be done, needs to be done, and should be done. When couples in troubled marriages do not consider time together to be good time for discussions, they will recognize once time has passed, it is gone forever.

Time lost is unredeemable. Couples concerned with resolving marital issues must understand that now is the best time to seek resolutions. Couples who take advantage of their shared time will spiritually evaluate their relationships. The depth of God's place in marriages often determine the ability of the relationship to endure difficult and troubled times. When God is missing in marriages, needed changes or adjustments are rarely made. Unfortunately, many such marriages remain on the road to divorce. Marriages which lack clear understanding between couples about unresolved issues and reasons why their relationship is dissolved, they will be left with the question, "Where did we go wrong?"

Peter and Gloria's love for each other kept their troubled marriage from becoming a marital statistic. Their relationship could serve as an example for couples thinking of getting divorced. They learned that true love, genuine love, and compromising love helped them to endure marital struggles. It enabled them to remain together rather than quit. Their relationship continued because they deemed their marriage to be a precious commitment in which they highly valued.

The strength of marriage is love. It is the committed process of combining two human lives, with personal differences, into a bonded relationship. These differences at times may seem strident and difficult to maintain. However, before divorce becomes the only solution which couples consider, they should examine their hearts, minds, and attitudes. Personal attitudes at times get in the way of common courtesy and compromised considerations. Negative attitudes must not be so pervasive among couples that they will not entertain marital compromises or be willing to work through differences. The right motivation for which couples may address their troubled marital relationships is for them to make love the center of all their struggles. Love will help them to better understand each other, teach them how to live together, and will help them avoid moments where divorce is the final word.

Peter and Gloria's story of love is no different than other married couples. They've faced challenges and marital difficulties which tested their commitment to stay together.

Marital bonding is both physical and spiritual connection. Through this joining process couples are aided by God's presence to build their lives together. Regardless of what some people or philosophy may aspire, marriage is not always an easy process of blending two lives into one loving relationship. Marriage is not a one-size-fit-all format for a successful engagement nor is it a finished product. It is a work in progress. That is why couples need an in-depth understanding of what is required of married life before they commit to being married. Marriage is a sacred spiritual connection between men and women which should not be taken lightly or treated insincerely. Its bonding elements will become strong enough that the relationship will endure through marital troubles, problems, or other issues. This spiritual bonding will prevent couples from dismissing or discarding marriage as a bad idea and divorce becomes the accepted way out.

Chapter 24

"Love and Happiness"

Oliver and Sandra's marital relationship was coming to an end. Divorce seemed to be their best outcome. The love they shared as childhood sweethearts appeared not to have been enough to keep them together. The little happiness they shared when their marriage began seemed like fleeting moments of emotions. The love they desired in their marriage appeared unreachable. The experiences of their past lives left them with too many uncertainties and conflicts. Yet, they both longed for that special kind of lasting love. The kind of love that would not put restrictions or restraints on the marriage. They needed a love that could be trusted and would hold their marriage together. However, Oliver's unfaithful past was often the concern and major reason for their marital conflicts. Although it was not true, he often blamed Sandra for his deviant behavior. He justified himself by accusing her of being unfaithful as was his previous wife. Sandra felt boxed-in a love-needed relationship. Regardless of what she did or did not do, he blamed her for his wrong actions. The marriage became too much for her to manage peacefully. She was not used to being attacked, abused, and always blamed for his actions. He was supposed to be her helper, provider, comforter, and lover. She didn't want to do it, but divorce seemed to be her best outlet for peace, safety, and relief.

Where did we go wrong? This valid question challenges every couple's break-up, and every broken marriage which seems irreparable. One of the easiest things to do in troubled marriages or strident relationships is to quit. It doesn't take much to quit. Quitting involves giving up. Quitting will not sufficiently face challenges which threaten the marital relationship. In some troubled relationships it is believed it best to let go and not stay connected to something or someone going nowhere. They conclude that staying isn't worth setbacks, abuse, or unproductive interactions. Sometimes, it is best to shut the shop down, close the windows, lock the doors, and move on. Sometimes, the desire to rekindle old flames is a mistake that won't hold a brighter candlelight. Especially if the relationship becomes saturated with negative issues, problems, and bad behaviors. It is best to leave a broken marriage with integrity than to remain in a relationship hampered with regrets, disappointments and failures.

Oliver and Sandra's marital struggles, which they shared through tears of regrets and disappointments, had dissolved. Hope for their marriage seemed a lost cause. They were ready to quit, give up, toss in the proverbial towel, call it a day, get a divorce. When surprisingly, Oliver interrupted the process with a genuine expression of his love. He apologized. What happened? What changed? Was this a ploy? Could this gesture be real? It was as if he saw heaven opened and he saw the face of God. Oliver got down on his knees, confessed his faults before God and asked Sandra for her forgiveness. He asked her for another chance to show his love for her and how he valued her as his wife. He acknowledged his need for her in his life. Reaching out his hand he touched her hand and pledged to never let go. He further promised to love her and never again compare her with anyone else. His pledges and promises became a prayer for acceptance. He wanted Sandra to believe in him and his love for her. He wanted her to feel the freedom and desire to blossom as the woman of beauty he had always thought her to be. Sandra was moved with compassion for Oliver after hearing these kind words coming out of his mouth. This man, Oliver, who had tortured her with ridicule and debasing words. Standing up and facing him,

Sandra placed her hands gently on his face touching him in a tender loving manner.

Sandra embraced Oliver with loving arms. This assured him that she forgave him and accepted his love. She made it clear to him that all she ever wanted was his love. His true love. The love she remembered him giving her years ago. His genuine love which shaped her heart to know what true love felt like. She admitted that she never wanted to divorce him. She wanted him in her life for always. She felt that the major problem which troubled their marriage was his efforts to prove to her that he could give her the world. His obsession was motivated by his feeling that he had to compete with her dead husband. Although her dead husband made her feel like a queen, she was now his to be made a queen. Sandra's deceased husband, during his life, made some smart investments which caused him to become a very wealthy man. He was not a rich man but had enough money to live comfortably and go places. Therefore, Oliver, feeling the competitive pressure, tried to show Sandra that he too could shower her with gifts, things, and have access to lots of money. He wanted her to know that he was able to give her everything she desired. More importantly, he wanted to make her feel secure and loved.

Sandra tried often to convince Oliver that she wasn't looking for things to make her happy or complete. She was looking for a man who would love and appreciate her. Oliver with his head against her chest cried tears of joy. He confessed that his previous marriage had broken him into many pieces of doubts, bitterness, and resentment. So, he wasn't sure that he could trust his heart to anyone to fix broken pieces and put them together again. He felt deceived many times before by scheming women who pretended he was Priority One in their lives. Only to discover at later times that these women wanted him for their own pleasures, his money, occasional sex, and a house they could come to when needed. These relationships left him longing for satisfaction, completion, and a woman's love he could trust. His search was empty and pointless until the day Sandra came back into his life. Her presence and involvement in his life changed him. Her bright spirit and pleasant personality brought sunshine to his world. However, his response to her positive influence toward him was cloaked within being cautious and reserved. He didn't know what he could do or should do to show his appreciation for her being the woman he had longed to have in his life. Instead, he placed her alongside all the other disappointing women he had come to know. Fortunately for Oliver, the truth about Sandra opened his eyes. She was real, true, and honest. She could be trusted. Her love could be trusted. He could now appreciate this beautiful woman for being his wife and the love of his life.

Sandra was Oliver's renewed life. She brought back into his heart and mind love with precious memories. Although he had known her most of his life, for the first time he saw her as being more than a person he knew. She was the woman for him. The woman who would be able to fill all the emptiness within his heart. Sandra, he thought, was the woman for him. Although he made the mistake of leaving Sandra for another pretty-faced woman, he soon came to know that real beauty goes beyond being pretty. Oliver's pretty-faced woman left him. Her challenge was winning him away from Sandra. Having won this tug-of-war battle against Sandra, this pretty woman soon tired of Oliver, left him in pursuit another man who caught her attention.

Brokenhearted and distraught, Oliver was ready to give up on love. His resolved attitude became one of which his pursuits in the game of love became the same as the women who played with his affection. He was willing to be phony in love, deceitful in practice, and untrue about a planned future with them. However, when Sandra came into his life things changed for him. His way of thinking about women changed. What he saw in Sandra made him want to be better. He needed someone to help him to be better. Sandra's love revived him.

Sandra never forgot about Oliver. Even after he abandoned her for another woman. Hurt and confused as to why their relationship ended. She felt nothing but pain. Nevertheless, Sandra's love for Oliver would not allow this breakage to stop her from caring about him. This woman who had become a distant thought in his love life, had now become the woman he needed once again. He needed what she most offered to him, her true love. Oliver realized that Sandra's kind heart and loving personality was needed to mend his broken heart. Sandra knelt lovingly beside Oliver and embraced this life-changing moment with him. God in this moment changed a man's bitterness into kindness. He changed an insecure lover into a faithful man who would love his wife. Because of this life-changing moment in Oliver's life, he adjusted his attitude toward Sandra. Asked for her forgiveness. Embraced a new concept toward partnership which included God. These many changes were the main reasons their marriage was restored.

Oliver, while on both knees, bowed his head in humble submission to God. He gave thanks for God having blessed him with another opportunity to have love, joy, and peace. He was thankful that his home would no longer be empty, broken, or fractured. He realized that this was an epiphany moment in his life. This spiritual change which had come over him healed his marital hurt. God provided him relief through Sandra's love. This change gave him confidence to disengage himself from his marital insecurities. It was Sandra's love and kindness who gave Oliver strength to face his weaknesses and shortcomings. Oliver's self-esteem and self-worth were deeply damaged by his previous marital relationship. Trust became a hindering concern. God's presence in their lives allowed Oliver and Sandra to restore and repair their broken marriage. God healed Oliver's damaged self-image through Sandra's love.

Oliver had always thought Sandra to be a beautiful woman. However, it was not until now that he realized her beauty was a genuine reflection of her person and personality. Sandra was not a self-absorbed person or a vain woman because of her beauty. She didn't think beauty was something for attention getting, instead, she thought that every woman should be valued for herself. She didn't mind being complimented for her beauty, but she neither sought any nor expected such to be given. The reality for her was that rejection had caused her not to consider herself as being physically appealing. It was her faith in God, not her physical appearance which gave her confidence to believe in herself. Her faith in God helped her through difficult and troubled times. Sandra's kindness was often seen or felt through her humility. It was not unusual for her to give other people greater consideration or allow them to go ahead of her. She never compared her looks or appearance to other women. Beauty was not her vanity. Nevertheless, Sandra, this beautiful woman, gave to Oliver her genuine care, sincerity, and a new outlook.

Sandra recognized that this shared time between them was sacred. Words were not needed. She reached out to him and embraced him with her loving arms. The smile on her face affirmed the fact that she was aware that something had changed within him. Her hope would be that this change would bring their lives together again. The questions they needed to answer about their marital relationship was, 'Where did we go wrong?' Nevertheless, they were thankful for the opportunity to restore their marriage. This meant allowing God to have a special place in their marriage. With God's presence in their marriage, He would be able to help them better love and connect with each other. God's presence would provide them strength needed to mend that which was broken. Because of this renewed connection, their love was reignited. They made a commitment to never use, apply, or echo the word divorce again.

Oliver and Sandra' marital relationship serve as evidence for other couples considering divorce. Marital conflicts, without loving considerations, could lead to separation. Their restored marriage proves that hope for renewal may prevent divorce from being the final word. It is on this accord that married couples seeking answers for their troubled relationships should think what outcome would be best for their marriages. Divorce should not be the only considered outcome. Reinforced marital relationships begin with affirming that marriage is a spiritual union. Marriage was ordained by God to be lifelong relationships between men and women. After God created the first couple, Adam and Eve into this holy union, He commanded them to "Be fruitful, and multiply," (Genesis 1:28a, KJV). Therefore, if marriage is perceived by uniting couples to be a holy union, they will embrace God's love and stay together.

Chapter 25

"Working Through Conflicts"

Unfortunately, there are many couples in troubled marriages who have accepted divorce as being their only option. In their present conditions they do not have peace, love, or a feeling of security. These relationships have endured, on numerous occasions, personal injuries, demeaning mental abuse, physical hardships, conflicts, and other unacceptable behaviors. Marriages for these troubled couples no longer resemble or reflect relationships which once were intended to be loving engagements. Marital conflicts often bring personal discouragements, broken spirits, and a desire to quit to escape the pains of failure. Conflicts alone do not reflect what marriages were meant to be. Marriage was never meant to be a binding burden or a chain of despair to engaged couples. Therefore, neither person nor couple living in abusive marriages should be required, encouraged, demanded, or expected to remain in such habitation.

Abuse! Whether it is physical, mental, psychological, or spiritual should be identified and named for what it remains to be, abuse! It should not, no! It must not be tolerated or accepted as normal behavior at any levels of human interactions. Men and women sharing love relationships need caring hearts, not abusive terror. For this reason, alone, men and women deciding to get married should know that the marital concept for couples is for them to build up, and not tear down or destroy one another. Marriage is the commitment to shared love which provides them with joy and satisfaction.

Marriage is a focused efforts which unite man and woman in forever love embraces. It is a union shaped through common bonds of shared visions. It is a partnership which builds relationships on the sacred concept that love is to be valued. It is a joyful union which thrives as couples employ themselves in love to be lovable. Each loving moment in marital relationships becomes shared treasured memories. Happiness and laughter fill the atmosphere of their homes. Visitors feel welcome.

A happy home occurs in marriages when couples spend time loving each other. A happy marriage permits each partner to be him/herself. Happiness will provide the sweet spirit of acceptance without applying efforts to reframe, remake, or change either partner. A happy home is where people care enough about each other to be happy.

Marriage is a precious process by which couples build their lives together. It is for a lifetime of love, laughter, sexual pleasures, and personal enjoyments. Through these four areas, communication, finances, sex and intimacy, family and friends, discussions have been made to utilize these elements for marital success and enrichment. With these elements couples' relationships are shaped into lasting loves through a shared purpose and destiny. These suggestive elements provide for marital success when couples engage in the process. Love keeps couples together, spiritually guided, and hearts united.

Chapter 26

"Quiet Stream Romances"

Falling in love is the effect of physical attractions, emotional desires, and spiritual needs to bond with someone. Love is personal and life changing. Falling in love is a process which makes the heart, mind, and spirit vulnerable to emotional disappointments. It is considered natural for two people to fall in love. As a matter of fact, culturally speaking, people are encouraged to find someone deemed special enough to partner with and fall in love. However, as much as falling in love is emphasized for partnership and lasting relationship, many couples often come short of this expectation. Instead, many find themselves settling for sweet sounding words about love and glamorous expensive gifts perceived to be acts of love. Whenever couples come together without being motivated by love, they usually substitute their unfulfilled moments with other things of interest. Such interests will often be based on wealth, positions, or possessions they have acquired. This substitution for lack of an amorous relationship will focus on having the appearance of happiness. Falling in love is important for marital relationships. It is equally essential in one's personal relationship with God. Falling in love with God provides the spiritual encirclement of faith, peace, love, and self-esteem. Falling in love with God provides spiritual qualities of care and concern.

God is omnipresent. He is everywhere at the same time. He is not limited to a specific place or time. God is in the church. He is outside the church. Although not every place is thought to be sacred, the church is a holy and sacred domain. The church is a place of reverence whereby the heart, mind, and spirit are renewed, refreshed, and restored. Similarly, The Quiet Stream (a fictional spiritual place) is deemed to be sacred. This Quiet stream, a spiritual place of refuge, is where troubled and conflicted couples come to find relief from their sorrows, hurts, failures, and defeats. For those seeking solitude, it is a place where they can come to meditate, think, or pray. It is an expectant place where restoration, self-evaluation, and spiritual renewal occur. Many times, couples would come, bringing their broken, and fragile relationships to the Quiet Stream. Through tears of repentance, they would reaffirm their heart-felt love for each other. Time at the Quiet Stream impacts couples' love for each other. It provides intimate moments which bring truth, meaning, purpose, and renewal to their marital relationships. The Quiet Stream is spiritual. It enshrines God's presence and power to mend broken hearts and change lives.

The Quiet Stream's influence on individuals or couples is not a power which dictates their behaviors or actions. Its purpose is to be a sacred space for moments of solitude and personal assessments. It becomes for couples a place for refreshed love, genuine expressions, and shared intimate moments. Its location cannot be found on any maps. It is not a resort or love haven setting that you can run to. Yet it is as real as any place where people seek for and find love, peace, and happiness. Its true location is found in every heart where love exists. It helps to rebuild and strengthen love relationships through bitter and troubling times. The Quiet Stream provides spiritual restorations. It has the capability for repairing brokenness, renewing optimism, and standing against attitudes which seek to destroy relationships.

The Quiet Stream is in a myriad of holy places, such as a personal praying ground, a church altar, a cathedral chapel, or a loving bedroom. Places wherever people seeking love and happiness may be found. However, for those who refuse to believe or accept the need to have God in their relationships, it is nothing more than a fantasy.

Those who seek to use its presence for personal or sensuous gratification will only find imitations of love with empty promises of happiness. However, those who understand the importance of having God's presence in marriages receive love and fulfillment at The Quiet Stream. Through God's presence and applied spiritual principles troubled relationships will be able to endure periods of disagreements, disappointments, and disgusts. God's presence in marriages will give couples support during troubled, divisive, and confusing marital times. The Quiet Stream has always been the place where couples seeking spiritual healing would gather. From the grasp of broken relationships, damaged self-images, and the need to feel loved, its power to heal and deliver remains the magnet of attraction. It has always been the place where spiritual intimacy deepens shared love. The Quiet Stream provides couples intimate moments and opportunities for them to celebrate love, joy, and second chances.

The Quiet Stream has always been the place where couples shared spiritual moments, meditations, and renewed love relationships. Peter and Gloria were one such couple who were attracted to this place. It was here where they met, engaged the moments, and fell in love. Their love relationship became a Quiet Stream example for couples experiencing marital difficulties. Their shared story of the Quiet Stream's influence in their lives gave them reasons to trust love and being loved again. Brokenhearted and discouraged they often spoke of how being at the Quiet Stream had mended their troubled minds, healed their broken hearts, and restored their desire for a loving companion. The Quiet Stream's method of spiritual and marital renewal provided many couples second chances for love and success. Second chances are not always available or easily achieved. Especially, after couples have been exposed to infidelity, wrestled with dishonesty, felt betrayed, and have had to tolerate other marital pains. Divorce for many couples has been the suggested outcome.

Chapter 27

"Second Chances"

Second chances often refer to opportunities given to correct wrongs, adjust adverse conditions, change undesired behaviors, and demonstrate better situational perspectives. Struggling marriages which apply spiritual influences and godly principles when engaging in battles for survival, will often create second chances for themselves. True-hearted lovers are valuable and trustworthy. False-hearted lovers are full of deceit. That is why choosing someone to love requires more than outward appearances or smooth speaking love languages. Outward appearances alone will not fulfill the spiritual desire for loving relationships. Loving relationships worthy of engaging and maintaining are graciously tempered with kindness, tenderness, devotion, and personal respect. It could be that the person you see may not be the real person you aspire to know, love, and adore.

Rather, that person may be a false-hearted lover whose motive is to steal the essence of your being and leave you longing for true love. Such a person's true intentions, before you get to know him/her, may be to deceive for sexual pleasures. This kind of person will display you with a false image of being a true lover to not reveal his/her true motivation. This imposter of love will practice deception of his/her real person or personality until after the marriage has occurred.

Lasting relationships are usually not associated with quick engagements. Enduring love is often seasoned with patience. This loving patience affords couples time to know each other before commitments are made. This loving patience will cause you to enjoy holding hands and sharing laughter before kisses are shared. This loving patience will wait through short journeys before long-term plans are made. This loving patience will seek true affections before sexual moments are engaged. That is why patience needs to be lovers' cautionary guide as they build lasting relationships. Getting to know a person requires knowing about that person. Getting to know a person involves learning about his/her likes and dislikes. It begins with honest conversations and shared explanations. It is the process of loving and being loved. Having good character speaks highly of the person. It usually reflects whether that person is real, honest, respectful, and kind. Getting to know the person seeking your love and affection is important because you need to know if promised love can be trusted. Therefore, couples should be patient in their relationship so that love would embrace their hearts and marriage becomes their goal. Marriage with an expected long-term commitment must be deeply rooted in truth and genuine love.

Having attractions for a person, being around a person, having background knowledge of the person, and even having shared intimate time with a person will not guarantee that you truly know that person. People generally show you what they want you to see and know about them. Only the parts which they feel safe and secure in themselves will be revealed. However, when negative secrets are exposed about a partner's history, disappointments will question whether you truly know that person. When secrets are based in deception marriages will become troubled and strained relationships.

A sure way to avoid marriages from becoming a past tense relationship is for couples, during courtship, to be patient and learn about one another. Learn his/her traits, habits, irritations and agitations. Don't allow assumptions to ruin the beauty of loving the one that you are with. Each person must seek to know his/her partner's various moods and understand how to respond when mood swings occur. Whether the mood is a need for quiet moments or loud bursts of screams which may be attributed to stress, tiredness, anger, or resentment. In either case perhaps the best remedy is to provide your loving partner some intimate attention and/or personal time. It is necessary for couples to know their partner's moods and respond appropriately. This understanding will prevent any misunderstandings which may cause the other partner to react inappropriately. This awareness will serve as the proper mechanism for avoiding or creating conflicts, altercations, or hurtful sayings.

Communication bridges the gaps between being informed and uninformed about the person who has captured your heart, warmed your feelings, and stirred up your most intimate thoughts. This understanding gives appreciation for this person who fills your empty heart with tender words of kindness and engaging love embraces. Understanding remains the major element for keeping married couples lovingly together.

Chapter 28

"The Closer I Get to You"

Couples' efforts to restore joy in their damaged marriages or repair broken relationships must be willing to share this journey together by refocusing their time and attention on one another. They need quiet personal places to work things out. Such places could include couples' retreats, romantic getaways, long awaited vacations, or just some private times together. Without asserting intentional efforts to change outlooks, perspectives, results of past failures, hurts and disappointments, these images of sorrows will remain hindering obstacles in this restoration process. Often, brokenness and being brokenhearted are painful and difficult entities for relationships to overcome or let go. However, restoration comes through couples' willing efforts to mend their broken hearts.

Music and songs have always been ways by which feelings, hurt, and pain were made known for recovery and healing of hearts. Among the many channels used to address broken hearts is the impact of songs. British singer and songwriter Robin Gibbs of the brothers' singing group, the Bee Gees, entertained the question of mending the broken heart in this song, 'How Can You Mend a Broken Heart.' The song includes these words, "I can think of younger days when living for my life was everything a man could want to do. I could never see tomorrow. I was never told about tomorrow. And how can you mend a broken heart? How can you stop the rain from falling down? Tell me, how can you stop the sun from shining? What makes the world go round? How can you mend this broken man? Yeah, how can a loser ever win? Somebody please help me mend my broken heart and let me live again."

Couples seeking help in restoring love, peace, and happiness in their marriages often reach out for people's opinions and suggested options. They usually find that opinions, and everyone has one or two, provide them little assistance in resolving their marital issues. Those couples seeking options other than divorce usually travel many paths and trails seeking solutions before realizing that having God in their marriages remains their best option for marital restorations. Marriages which employ God's principles of love, duty, respect, and partnership find strength for survival in God's word. This spiritual support does not exclude them from the same struggles as those who ignore God. It does give them the assurances of God's promises to help, guide, and support them through their troubles. Marital relationships are strengthened by couples' love and desire to please one another. These closely joined love relationships provide couples the ability to endure every challenge, trial, struggle, or opposition they face. It draws them closer to each other in mind, heart, and spirit which form a loving bonding them together.

Grammy Award winner Roberta Flack, along with Donny Hathaway, in their romantic ballad, "The Closer I Get to You," provides encouragement to lovers everywhere who not only want to love the one that they are with, but also know how to stay with that loved one. The words to their medley include the following: "The closer I get to you, the more you make me see. By giving me all you got, your love has captured me. Over and over again I tried to tell myself that we could never be more than friends and all the while inside I knew it was real, the way you make me feel. Lying here next to you time just seems to fly. Needing you more and more let's give love a try. Sweeter than sweeter love grows and heaven's there for those who fool the tricks of time, with the hearts of love they find true love in a special way. The closer I get to you the feeling comes over me, pulling closer, sweet as the gravity to you. The closer I get to you, the more you make me see. By giving me all you got, your love has captured me."

Love! True love! Energetic love! Long lasting love! These expressions help us to know and understand that love is more than moments of pleasure. Love is greater than feelings of ecstasy. Love is more enduring than sentimental thoughts. Love is the passion which motivates times lived, times shared, and times treasured with one another. Love is the forgiving element in marriages gone wrong. It is the salvage net which catches and reserves valued moments. It is a sustaining reasoning which overlooks hurt and hides a multitude of faults. Marriages, immersed in love, are not insulated from problems and troubles. It will, as with all other relationships, encounter struggles and growing pains. However, the differences between marriages saturated with love, and marriages for other reasons than love is that when problems come, love will keep one marriage together, while the one lacking love will want out. They will call it quits.

Couples motivated by love strive harder, work longer, and feel more secure. Long term marriages require commitment filled with genuine love and sincere affections. When marriages are based on outward attractions, physical appearances, or possessions of wealth, and not on love, couples in troubled times will be tempted and pressured to quit. Marriages strengthened by love can endure tough times.

Chapter 29

"Confirmed Marriages"

Peter and Gloria loved each other. This love helped them avoid having their marriage end in divorce. Although their many struggles baited them to end it all, such struggles taught them to value and love their marriage. They learned that having a good marriage will not insulate couples from personal conflicts, troubling issues, or financial difficulties. Neither will it prevent discontentment from becoming negative comments, or focused blames or hurtful accusations. It will not keep foolish gossip from interrupting passionate moments of intimacy. These marital disrupters are purposed to erode couples' feelings of joy, peace, happiness and leave them empty of love. When these and other volatile occurrences happen, the easiest thing to do is to look for a way out of relationships. There came a time in the marriage of Peter and Gloria when such temptations to quit or give up were serious considerations. They could have quit, divorced, gone their separate ways, and justified their decision as having tried. Instead, they chose to battle through their marital issues and stayed together. It was not because they were so strong that they didn't need anything or anyone. Nor were they so determined to make it work that they wouldn't let their relationship end, or marriage fail. It was because they recognized their weaknesses and inability to sustain their marriage and shared love. It was at that point of realization that they sought help from counselors. They found that it was God's love in their marriage that they most needed. After heeding the advice of spiritual counselors, they agreed that it was God who brought them together. If they were to last, God's presence would be needed to keep them together.

The time had come for another financial workshop seminar which would again be conducted by Reverend Jerry Seay. Peter and Gloria received personal invitations to attend. Having attended the seminar before, they were special guests. They remembered how much they benefited from their first seminar. It helped them to understand the value of achieving financial independence. They happily agreed to attend. They remembered how important it was for them to learn the benefits of financial management. Peter and Gloria, knowing how helpful this financial information is for struggling marriages, invited two other couples to go with them. The invited couples were Stan and Maria, along with Oliver and Susan. Peter and Gloria were excited about having their new friends to go with them.

After arriving at the seminar, Peter and Gloria realized that the seminar was structured differently this time. Their first seminar was an auditorium setting. The audience sat politely in their seats and took notes as the lecturer spoke and presented the information. This session was structured for interactive small groups participation. In these groups, couples were instructed to focus their discussions and topics on how to effectively organize, prioritize, and manage their household finances. Prior to the seminar, organizers of the event utilized collected data on effective ways to conduct seminars and workshops to best serve attendees. The collected information indicated that small groups' participation would more effectively benefit couples lacking sufficient financial and money management skills. Although couples would differ in their approach to gaining financial and management skills, they all would share the similar need of understanding the best method for household management. The event Organizers wanted seminar participants to understand that the small discussion groups were not designed for them to imitate another couple's marriage, nor decide to manage their finances in ways that others did theirs. This interactive seminar was structured for couples to hear and be introduced to various financial options which best supported their own situations. Couples were cautioned to understand that what worked well in one couple's house was not guaranteed to work well in other houses.

The seminar's small groups format proved to be a valuable method by which couples were encouraged to talk about their marital mishaps and financial mismanagements. It gave them opportunities to discuss their misunderstandings of shared partnership and their misapplied logic for handling money. One major problem that couples revealed about their marital experiences was their inability to effectively communicate with each other. They shared their difficulties in understanding how they were to live and express themselves. They spoke openly about how they questioned their marital living. They agreed that perhaps their considered greatest mishaps or failures they encountered as couples were trying to operate without an operating plan. Inventor and Statesman Benjamin Franklin said, "If you fail to plan, you are planning to fail."

Peter and Gloria did not view themselves as being leaders of the group they were in, nor marital examples for others to emulate, but the other couples looked up to them. As the general discussion of marital issues continued with each small group, Rev. Seay, moderator of the seminar, challenged the small group couples to participate in a specific exercise designed to help them to be truthful in their responses to each other. He first asked the men, with their wives facing them, to take their wives hands into their hands and draw their wives closer to them. This closeness, he explained, should be to the point that the men would be looking directly into the faces and eyes of the women. Peter, taking the lead, made the first move. He took Gloria by her hands and gently pulled her close to him. He smiled at her as he held that pose. Stan hesitated to follow this lead because he felt uncomfortable. He was not the kind of man that openly displayed affections in public. Hesitantly, he took Maria's hands, and he too gently pulled her close to him. In this awkward moment of personal space invasion, he noticed with loving appreciation, the smoothness of his wife's facial skin. The glinting curiosity in her eyes comforted him in this awkward setting. On the other hand, it was not a problem for Oliver to hold Sandra's hands or pull her close to him. His way of thinking was that the closer they were together, the better their lives would become. After being in that position for a short period of time, Stan and Oliver questioned the next moves or positions for this exercise. Peter waited patiently. After a few minutes, Rev. Seay asked the men whether they were tired of holding their wives' hands? Were they satisfied in just holding hands? Could their wives see or perceive love and appreciation in their faces as they held their hands? Before he allowed them to answer these almost rhetorical questions, he turned the attention towards their wives. Ladies, he asked, while your husbands are holding your hands, do you feel secure in their grasps? Do you feel loved or possessed? While he holds your hands do you hold him right back? Again, before you answer these questions, think about what roles these connections have in securing your marriages. He moved away to allow for more group interactions.

Couples in Peter and Gloria's small group had an advantage over some of the other groups because they knew each other prior to attending this event. However, what these couples needed most was straightforward discussions on how to become better managers of their finances. Peter and Gloria welcomed the opportunity to share with others what they learned through their financial struggles, which taught them how to be better managers of their monies. They didn't hesitate to emphasize to the group the importance of having God at the center of all their marital discussions and considerations. They also included the need for couples to have strong spiritual bonds established between them, so that with God's help, they will stay together. Peter told them that when he and Gloria wrestled through their financial struggles, they found strength and support from concerned Christian counselors who guided them to successful money management.

As with the previous seminar which Peter and Gloria attended, this one also provided couples with valuable financial information designed to help couples better manage their finances. Couples need to understand Ecclesiastes 10:19 which states "A feast is made for laughter, and wine maketh merry: but money answereth all things," (KJV).

This seminar provided attendees with practical teachings on financial principles and applying spiritual guidelines. Reverend Seay, the seminar lecturer, continued to emphasize the importance of keeping God in all marital discussions. He told them that God needs to be the center of all their plans and planning. He encouraged them to seek God for their personal lives and spiritual strength for their marriages. He told them that keeping God centered in the marriage was essential to couples' understanding, cooperation, and ability to work together and to maintain their marriages. He reminded them to never forget to include God in all their plans. Again, he pointed out that giving was the essential part of financial gains. He stated that contrary to how some people may think about giving and receiving, unlike those who refrain from giving to God, the financial benefits which couples may enjoy comes when the Godkind of giving becomes first part of financial management.

Peter and Gloria were a loving example of a happily married couple. Other couples in their group felt an attraction to them as they openly shared their relational experiences, marital challenges, and their commitment to faithfully remain together. Their genuine love, tenderness, and expressed happiness for each other was refreshing for them to see. Peter and Gloria's marital partnership was seen by other couples as the perfect example of concern and care. Their relationship displayed among the group stimulated discussions of how to keep love in marriages. As they talked among themselves, Stan and Maria sought answers to the question that had been like a hangnail in their marriage. They wanted to know how they could maintain a happy home in broken relationships.

As Peter began to discuss Stan and Maria requested topic, Reverend Seay overhearing the concern, interrupted. He was careful not to allow Peter to provide them with an answer. He knew the frailties of new friendships and relationships. Good and even intended good advice or suggestions by unqualified friends or family could end or greatly damage relationships if advice given goes wrong or becomes reasons for marriage failure. Therefore, he utilized this moment to help Stan and Maria provide their own understanding and commitment to marriages. He took them back to the personal exercise in which they participated. He reminded them that marriage is an up-close relationship. Couples are damaged when they allow personal issues to place loving and emotional distances between them. Reverend Seay emphasized that having marital happiness is more important than feelings or demanding occasions. Happiness is a commitment to finding joy in the person's life you share. Those moments which are special to you become smiles that keep you through the frowns of life. He reminded them that marital conflicts or heated discussions over issues and problems are not always indications of unhappiness or that happiness no longer exists. He challenged them to know that sometimes couples find more happiness with each other after going through difficulties and stormy situations. How can it be, you say? Well, in times of difficulties, people who love each other, care about each other, and want to build their lives together are drawn closer together. He told them that married couples learn a lot about each other when they work through issues. As Reverend Seay continued speaking, it was as though an awakening light was in their faces. Stan and Maria looked at each other with a greater sense of appreciation. They started talking to each other in ways which suggested that they had finally got the message and understanding they were seeking. The happiness they were trying to find, they had it all the time. Without feeling any embarrassment, Stan hugged Maria tightly and passionately kissed her in front of everyone. Afterwards, Stan turned to Reverend Seay and said to him, "Thank you, Sir!"

Chapter 30

"When The Grass Is Not Greener"

The small groups seminar turned out to be a productive format and an effective outlet for couples' discussions. Couples attending the seminar were able to share their experiences as well as receive answers to pertinent martial questions. They were able to learn valuable planning methods and effective money management ideas. The process of networking was introduced as a way for them to connect with various people whose influences, skills, knowledge and other relatable abilities, along with resources may help them achieve their goals. Friendships were also established and gained. For Peter and Gloria, this seminar was better than the one they previously attended. The concluding session of the seminar was interrupted by a surprise announcement. The organizers of the event quieted the seminar attendees who were busy collecting their belongings in preparation to leave. The event leader apologized to everyone for this last-minute insert, but they believed that this last presentation would be worthwhile for them who had come to the seminar. Couples were told that they needed to hear this presentation. Baffled by this last-minute activity, these couples didn't think that they needed to hear more than they had already learned. Nevertheless, the couples returned to their seats. Suddenly an elderly couple came into the room and were introduced to them. The expressions on many of the couples' faces questioned why they would need to listen to these old people. Out of respect they politely gave them their attention.

The old man spoke first and identified himself as John. His wife beside him was named Mary. He told the crowd that he and Mary had been at the seminar the whole session watching, listening, and observing couples' interactions with one another. They had waited until now for the opportunity to talk with them about love, care, and marital appreciation. Amid their personal concerns for the institution of marriage, John and Mary wanted these couples to hear their story of love and what almost cost them their marriage. Mary cautioned, in a tender caring mother-like voice, for couples not to take their love for granted or allow money to be their greatest concern. She told them that money is necessary to meet marital needs. However, there are other issues and concerns which they need to be aware that will affect them and could destroy their marriages. She warned them, "Don't be fooled by appearances. Every happy-looking couple is not as happy as they look. They've just learned how to play the game of pretending." John, interrupting, said, "You may think that because we are old, we have shared many happy years together. Well, let me tell you this, it could have been. However, because of poor choice-making and bad decisions mostly by me, it has not been." John paused for a long moment as he looked at the audience and noticed that he had their undivided attention. Though many couples in the session seemed baffled by this whole presentation. Peter and Gloria, Stan and Maria, Oliver and Sandra were wondering why they needed to hear some old couple's sad life story. They had been inspired, reinvigorated, and refocused on how to effectively manage their finances to build their home in love. For them, and many other couples, listening to John and Mary was like having their enthusiasm drowned out by a past that had nothing to do with them. John replaced the room silence with a heart-felt thanks to seminar couples for listening to them and hearing of their love plight.

Although John and Mary had been married (on paper) for more than 40 years, they came to this session celebrating their fifth renewed marriage anniversary. John told them that he and Mary's marriage experienced interruption due to infidelity and unfaithfulness. However, they were reunited and brought back together by the grace of God. "The main cause for our separation was betrayal of our marital vows to be loving and faithful to each other. Till death do we part." He said that these actions caused their relationship to fall apart. He made it painfully clear that this separation from Mary left him feeling alone. He was a lonely man. His behavior caused him to live away from the home which was once filled with love, joy, and happiness. It also made wherever he stayed feel like an empty house. The more he thought about what he lost through lustful enticements, the more his life became filled with sadness, emptiness, and hours of loneliness.

John, speaking words of regrets about his marital experiences and convictions, warned the men about the choices they make. He told them that "Bad decisions often yield worst consequences." He confessed that he found out that he was wrongly led into thinking that life would be better for him without Mary, rather than being with her. This decision caused him to leave the most important person a desperate man, such as he, always need which is a good woman and a faithful wife. John went on to share his story of love, separation, and love again. "You see," he said, "I left my wife for another woman. I allowed lust of the eyes to lead me to believe that grass on the other side was greener than the grass surrounding my marriage." He paused at what could be called a 'pregnant moment' before he spoke again, "I hurt my wife. I dishonored our home. I made bad decisions. Ten years away from home, my life went from riches to rags. My newfound friends turned out to be my worst enemies. They were nothing more than leeches robbing me of all my wealth. I found myself feeling like the Prodigal Son of the Bible, lost in a strange land."

Mary put her arms around John's shoulders and whispered in his ear, "Honey, it's my turn to share the other side of our love story." She turned to the audience and spoke in a kind, yet bold determined voice with a caring message and marital advice. She said, "What I am about to say is primarily for all the wives here who want to keep your husbands for a lifetime." Mary's statement caused all the wives to sit up straight in their seats as though to say, "What are you talking about?" Mary continued, "Ladies, if you want to have a marriage that will always satisfy your longings and will meet your every need, then what I'm about to say is important for you to know, practice, and commit to. When it comes to your marriage, don't ever give up on your man. I know that some of you may chuckle over this advice, but please don't misunderstand me about the seriousness of what I am saying. I want to caution you about your responsibility as wives to make your marriages last. Don't take what I am saying lightly. I am old, but certainly not stupid. I have three main pieces of advice for you to consider. The First piece of advice is this, don't let your marriages be controlled by outside influences that's always putting your man down or pointing out your man's faults. My Second piece of advice is that you don't be one who is quick to jump to conclusions without giving him a chance to explain his actions. My Third piece of advice asks for your patience. There may come a time in your relationship when your husband will appear to lose interest in you and stray in another woman's direction. However, if he is not abusing you physically, psychologically, or mentally, don't you dare think about leaving him or threaten to go out of that door. Stay with your man! Instead, examine yourself! How appealing are you to you? If you can't attract interest in yourself, why should he be attracted to you? Now, I'm not excusing men in any way from keeping their vows to love, cherish, support, and protect you as their wives. There is no right in doing wrong. When a man leaves his wife for another, he is guilty of violating his promise to love you forever. He has failed to romance you in love.

Let me tell you about one of the most disheartening days and moments in my life. John and I had been married for more than 20 years. We were happy. At least I thought we were. We were building our lives toward a prosperous future where we would be able to relax and enjoy our lives when we became old. Without fair warnings or indications that our marriage was in danger of being destroyed, it happened. It left me unprepared. Quick as lightning, things changed for me in that flash. John came to me that dreadful day with tears in his eyes and told me that he didn't love me anymore. He said that he had found a new love. His new love interest was a woman he said who knew how to talk him up, and not beat him down. Who listened to what he had to say and not always telling him what to do. She was a woman who caressed him in tenderness and not one whose touch felt like sandpaper. He believed her to be the kind of woman he needed to live with the rest of his life and not one he couldn't wait to rid himself of. He then said to me, 'Thanks for the memories! I'm gone.' Just like that my world crashed. I wasn't given the opportunity to question the things he said, which came as a surprise. I was not aware of his unhappiness. I didn't know he felt that way about me. Stunned! Shocked! Perplexed! I wanted to cry, but why? What would be my reasoning? The man I loved who promised to live with until we die just walked out of my life. What would be my next move? What should I do?

Well, I want you to know that I did what I've always done when I needed to clear my mind. I turned to music. On this day the radio station was playing oldie Goldie songs by the Dells, a 1960s rhythm and blues group. Ironically the song played just happened to have been one of my favorites. The song was 'Stay in My Corner'. As I listened to this love ballad tears filled my eyes. The words stirred my heart "If you stay darling. Stay in my corner. You make me so proud. Stay darling, please stay. To the world I'd cry my love. How I love you. Honey, I love you, I really love you. Please, please, please stay darling. Stay in my corner. And I will never, never let you down. Just say you'll stay 'cause I'll need you always around to tell me you love me. Honey, you love me, so darling stay. There will be times when I fail. I'll need your love to sometimes comfort me. Bitter days may prevail, but just a kiss from you will make them sweet. So, stay! Stay darling! Stay in my corner." Unfortunately for me John was gone, and could not hear me say to him, 'darling, please stay.'

Marriage is an important connection. I found myself unable to function without my then disconnected partner. I felt helpless, hopeless, and without direction. At one point I thought about doing what he did, finding me someone else to love, but I couldn't. My heart belonged to one person. My vows destinated me to the man who I pledged to love. Therefore, I turned my feelings, affections, and disappointments over to the Lord. I needed strength greater than I possessed. As result of my efforts to seek spiritual peace, I was able to move forward with my life. I began facing each day with new appreciation of myself and the potentials for me to trust God for healing of my soul, mind, and heart. So, ladies I am asking you to take this from me. When troubles enter your marriages don't surrender it to anything but hope. Give God room in your situation to mend the broken, strengthen that which is weak, and trust Him to repair the bridge that will bring him back home."

Mary ended her part of the story with a look of affection for John. She asked these wives to stay true to their goals and desires for their marriages. She encouraged them to ask and answer this marriage saving question when their relationships are faced with issues which come to destroy their partnership. This should be done before any talks, discussions, or decisions to separate or divorce become the main marital disclaimer, 'where did we go wrong?'

Mary's final words of encouragement went this way, "There are many things we can point out which caused our marital struggles, but aside from that I want you all to know this one thing, I love my husband! I am so glad to have him back home." John with tears in his eyes, said aloud, "I am a blessed man." Then he revealed to the seminar participants their purpose and reason for sharing their story of love, separation, and renewed affection. John said to the audience, "Please allow me to share with you the greatest part of our precious love story. I am not ashamed to admit that Mary is the heart of our love relationship. Her genuine love for me and love for a better life have been a bright shining light which has been stronger than my darkness as a wayward husband. It attracted me to walk out of my dark situation and return to the light of Mary's love. It directed me out of the darkness and back into Mary's arms. Some may call our journey of renewal an act of fate. I believe it to be a testament of God's presence and a wife's committed love for her husband. I didn't deserve a second chance with this beautiful woman who loved me more than I demonstrated love her or myself. Without Mary in my life, I lost all my wealth. However, through God's grace I was given opportunity to live once again with a loving wife in a restored home, with a recommitted love, based on spiritual principles.

Because of our financial enrichment we asked for this special time with you all to encourage you to love each other and for you to love being married to one another. Therefore, we are providing each couple here with a special night out at our expense. It is an invitation to lovers who want to keep their love in the marriage they share. A financial voucher with an unlimited amount will be provided to each of you so that, at your choice, you may spend a loving evening together. The cost is on us. Our only request is that this time become an opportunity to share loving memories which will keep you together. In addition, one group among you has been selected for a week-long love cruise. We wish each of you happy and long-lasting marriages with happiness.

The group we have selected to go on the cruise will be rewarded for being ambassadors of love and marriage. During this cruise, it is our prayers that your relationships be further engaged, strengthened, supported by the care you have for each other. May your lives be filled with joy, love, laughter, and longevity." The small group which consisted of Peter and Gloria, Stan and Maria, Oliver, and Sandra was selected for this pleasure trip. All the couples at the seminar thanked the old couple for their generosity as they departed the seminar. The selected small group going on the cruise were more than grateful. They were jubilant. They embraced the old couple as they left the seminar.

Part 5

THE CONCLUSION
"Tell It Like It Is"

Chapter 31

No Love Like God's Love

Love is a gentle word filled with much tenderness. It conjures up feelings of belonging, attachment, and commitment. It possesses amorous power which is strong enough to turn sadness into joy, causes frowns to become smiles, and pulls sunshine through cloudy days. Love is the apple every lover seeks to bite. Love is God's intimate gift for men and women to embrace. There is no love like God's love. The Apostle Paul described the Godkind of love this way in I Corinthians 13:4-8 (NLT), "Love is patient and kind. Love is not jealous or boastful or proud. It does not demand its own way. It is not irritable, and it keeps no record of being wronged. It does not rejoice about injustice but rejoices whenever the truth wins out. Love never gives up, never loses faith, is always hopeful, and endures through every circumstance. Prophecy and speaking in unknown tongues and special knowledge will become use-less. But love will last forever."

For this cause marital couples should examine the ques-tion, "Where did we go wrong?" from the vantage point of determining whether the relationship still has room for restoration. It should also challenge each marital couple who may be thinking about separating to reconsider their focus before deciding to divorce. Truthful answers to this question will often help couples make the best decisions if not the right ones. It will also release them from the many fears, doubts, misunderstandings, and confusions which have penetrated their lives with unresolved prob-lems. However, on the bright side of this examination, couples who are willing to risk losing their marriages by being honest and sincere usually reap opportunities which enables them in saving their relationships. It will also allow them valuable time to restore their love. Couples having courage enough to honestly and sincerely address problem areas in their marriages usually find themselves being liberated from their many fears. This process is good for every troubled marriage. Laying it all on the prover-bial line may not always yield desired results, but it still needs to be done. It is best to have an honest answer early in the relationship rather than live with years of deceit. The answers to many marital problems in question may not secure or save some marriages and some may end in divorce. Issues which erode, and damage marital relationships often include the following: infidelity, lack of trust, unfaithfulness, and insincere expressions of love. At this stage of discussions and engagements, divorce, for such couples, seems the only decision.

Decisions bear consequences. Couples who engage in marriages without considering how married life works bear the consequences of disappointment. Couples who exploit the concepts of marriage for material benefits bear the consequences of marital disillusionment. Couples whose vision of marital living as being extensions of a beautifully choreographed wedding ceremony bear the consequences of life not being beds of roses.

Divorce doesn't always set couples free. The residual effects of marital failures can at times bring on depression and poor self-esteem for some couples. It can erode their future trust in any promises of love, commitment, or lasting relationships. Divorce for some may be perceived as an opportunity to start over again in the game of love. For others, divorce comes to represent an end to love or having someone to love.

Contrary to those who have given up on investing in love again after divorce, because of heart-felt pains, love can be trusted, and hearts can be restored. Love remains the healing balm needed for those hurting from marital failures. The Godkind of love is required for maintaining lasting relationships. Without this spiritually influenced love, all relationships become candidates for emotional abuse, sexual misuse, lustful indulgence, and empty feelings. When love is defined only through human emotions lovers will always find disappointment at the end of the rainbow. True love includes a spiritual connection which makes God the centerpiece of the marital experience. God is love.

Marriage was ordained by God as a bonding engagement between men and women. When divorce occurs, it signifies couples' failure to remain spiritually attuned to their purposed connection and their marital vows to love one another. Therefore, when couples come to this road of disconnect, they need to examine and ask the question, 'where did we go wrong?'

There is no greater love story than the sacrifice of God's Son for the sins of the world. He willingly suffered humiliation, rejection, and abandonment so that we may have the fellowship with God in the beauty of holiness. This love made it possible for men and women to find warmth, comfort, and partnership in each other's bosom. Marriage is a beautiful celebration of this joining together of two lives to become one love. This spiritual bonding requirement is often substituted for good looks, strong muscles, and deep pockets leaving the relationship vulnerable to the possibility of failure. Without having deep spiritual roots of love in the heart, couples encountering marital adversity or dissension are more likely to look for a way out rather than reasons to stay. These conversations usually end with insinuations about divorce. When couples come to view divorce as a quick fix to their marital problems, they come to realize that divorce settlements are not always an equal opportunity agreement. Through effective marital counseling couples may realize that divorce is not a get out of a troubled marital relationship free card. Therefore, before divorce becomes the final statement each partner should be willing to admit their faults, flaws, and short-comings. Then with all sincerity and honesty ask with an inward answer to the question, 'Where did we go wrong?' Couples facing divorce must be willing to seek options before reaching this conclusion. Change can occur. People can do better. Marriages can survive difficult times, financial hardships, and other martial problems. When couples have genuine love and care for one another they will discover the needed energy within their marriages to again try building their lives together. Before the break-up, couples need to seek ways to make-up. One sure way begins with them asking and answering the question, "Where Did We Go Wrong?"

References

BeeGees, Barry, Robin and Maurice Gibbs (1971). "How Can You Mend A Broken Heart" Allmusic:Trafalgar: Charts& Awards: Billboard Albums." Retrieved 5 May 2013.

Dells, The, American R&B vocal group (1965). "Stay In My Corner."

Flack, Roberta (1972). "The First Time Ever I Saw Your Face." Atlantic Recording Corp., 1841 Broadway, New York, N.Y.

Flack, Roberta, & Hathaway, Donny (1978). "The Closer I Get To You." Atlantic Recording Corp., 1841 Broadway, New York, N. Y.

Guest, Edgar Allen (1921). Poem, Don't Quit. British-born, American poet.

Holy Bible, King James Version (KJV). Thompson Chain Reference Bible (2010), B.B. Kirkbride Bible Company, Inc., Indianapolis, In.

Holy Bible, New Living Translation (NLT) 1996. Tyndale Publishers, Inc. Wheaton, Illinois.

Seay, Jerry A., Pastor, Lecturer, Past President of Northwest District Convention, affiliated with Alabama State Missionary Baptist Convention.

Sledge, Percy (1968). R&B vocalist, "Take Time To Know Her." Atlantic Recording Corp., 1841 Broadway, New York, N. Y.

Stylistics (1973). R&B vocalists from Philadelphia, Pa. "Break Up To Make Up." Avco Records Corp. 1301 Avenue of Americas, New York.

Preface

Where did we go wrong? Where do we go from here? These challenging questions are often found attached to couples experiencing difficulties in their marriages. Before divorce becomes the final word in their relationships, couples are encouraged to examine their interest, motives, commitment, and personal interests to determine whether their marriages may be restored or maintained. Marriage is a sacred relationship institution. It is ordained by God and intended to be a bonding and binding lifetime connection. Men and women who seek lifetime partners to build their lives with need to know that marriage is not an isolated building process. There are loving and supporting family, friends, and acquaintances available to provide support and encourage positive marital development. The strength and weakness as well as the lasting or failure of marriages hinge on these four elements: Communication, Finances, Sex and Intimacy, and Family and Friends. Through each of these categories, couples must assess the proper use of them for their marital success. Where do we go from here? Is quitting an option? Is staying coward-ice? Will divorce provide relief? Or will it bring emptiness and loneliness? Couples must decide whether their rela-tionships and marriages are worth them investing the nec-essary time and understanding to intimately answer the question, Where Did We Go Wrong?

Acknowledgement

This book is dedicated to married couples who after facing many opportunities to leave to relationship, stayed and through loving commitment mended that which was broken.